SONGS *of* WISDOM

Growing Up Black: From Slave Days to the Present—
Twenty-five African Americans
Reveal the Trials and Triumphs of Their Childhoods

QUOTATIONS FROM FAMOUS

AFRICAN AMERICANS

OF THE TWENTIETH CENTURY

William Morrow and Company, Inc. / New York

Songs of Wisdom

Jay David

It is the policy of William Morrow and Company, Inc., and its imprints and affiliates, recognizing the importance of preserving what has been written, to print the books we publish on acid-free paper, and we exert our best efforts to that end.

Library of Congress Cataloging-in-Publication Data

Songs of wisdom : quotations from famous African Americans of the twentieth century / [compiled by] Jay David.—1st ed.
  p. cm.
ISBN 0-688-16497-8
1. Afro-Americans—Quotations.   I. David, Jay.
PN6081.3.S66   2000
973'.0496073—dc21   99-36058
CIP

Printed in the United States of America

First Edition

1   2   3   4   5   6   7   8   9   10

BOOK DESIGN BY JAM DESIGN

www.williammorrow.com

CONTENTS

Foreword / ix

Acknowledgments / xi

Childhood and Youth / 1

Identity / 13

Race Relations / 36

Civil Rights / 59

Education / 74

Religion / 80

The Military / 89

Politics / 92

Contents

Abortion / 100

Sports / 102

Skills / 109

The Arts / 112

Entertainment / 126

Opinions and Philosophies / 133

FOREWORD

The sojourn of African Americans in the twentieth century has been an unparalleled struggle, with excrutiating psychological and cultural conflicts arising at every turn. But there were also profound physical dangers that had to be faced every day, dangers within and outside the black community, threats that changed with each decade, from lynch mobs to the Ku Klux Klan to drugs to AIDS.

Through it all, African-American leaders, artists, and athletes have been astonishingly brave and eloquent, wise and witty, as this book so richly demonstrates.

A C K N O W L E D G M E N T

I very much appreciate Tom Steele's creative assistance in making this book possible.

SONGS *of* WISDOM

CHILDHOOD *and*

YOUTH

The world should not pass judgment upon the Negro, and especially the Negro youth, too quickly or too harshly. The Negro boy has obstacles, discouragements, and temptations to battle with that are little known to those not situated as he is. When a white boy undertakes a task, it is taken for granted that he will succeed. On the other hand, people are usually surprised if the Negro boy does not fail.

Booker T. Washington

About in late 1934, I would guess, something began to happen. Some kind of psychological deterioration hit our family circle and began to eat away at our pride. Perhaps it was the constant tangible evidence that we were destitute. We had known other families who had gone on relief. We had known without anyone in our home ever expressing it that we had felt prouder not to be at the depot where the free food was passed out. And now, we were among them. At school, the "on relief" finger was pointed at us, too, and sometimes it was said aloud. . . . Sometimes, instead of going home from school, I walked the two miles up the road into Lansing [Michigan]. I began drifting from store to store, hanging around outside where things like apples were displayed in boxes and barrels and baskets, and I would watch my chance and steal me a treat. You know what a treat was to me? Anything!

Malcolm X

It is really important that young people find something that they want to do and pursue it with passion. . . . I'm very passionate about filmmaking. It's what I love to do.

Spike Lee

Children have never been very good at listening to their elders, but they have never failed to imitate them.

James Baldwin

Children's talent to endure stems from their ignorance of alternatives.

Maya Angelou

At fifteen life had taught me undeniably that surrender, in its place, was as honorable as resistance, especially if one had no choice.

Maya Angelou

Even though your kids will consistently do the exact opposite of what you're telling them to do, you have to keep loving them just as much.

Bill Cosby

I truly believe that if ever a state social agency destroyed a family, it destroyed ours. We wanted and tried to stay together. Our home didn't have to be destroyed. But the welfare, the courts, and the doctor gave us the one-two-three punch. And ours was not the only case of this kind.

I knew I wouldn't be back to see my mother again [in the State Mental Hospital at Kalamazoo, Michigan] because it could make me a very vicious and dangerous person—knowing how they had looked at us as numbers and as a case in their book, not as human beings. And knowing that my mother in there was a statistic that didn't have to be, that existed because of a society's failure, hypocrisy, greed, and lack of mercy and compassion.

Malcolm X

I never had a chance to play with dolls like other kids. I started working when I was six years old.

Billie Holiday

There is no obstacle in the path of young people who are poor or members of minority groups that hard work and preparation cannot cure.

Barbara Jordan

We are now in a period where society is going to have to grow up and face the kinds of flaws that people have, who may in fact be important people. . . . Young people are often cynical because every historical figure in America wasn't a perfect person. For example, Thomas Jefferson owned slaves, so his writing of the Declaration of Independence doesn't mean anything. When I would talk to black kids who were so irritated by the various flaws they found in certain white historical figures, and they'd say, "We want to reject all that and find something that's pure and real," I would ask them had they ever heard of William Shockley, and the answer would invariably be no. And I said, "You know William Shockley is an arch, dyed-in-the-wool, redneck, racist, scumbag dog of the sort you're talking about. He also is one of the three guys who got the Nobel Prize for inventing the transistor." And I said, "I truly do wish you would reject him and his product—because then we wouldn't have to put up with them God damn boom boxes."

Stanley Crouch

I love to see a young girl go out and grab the world by the lapels. Life's a bitch. You've got to go out and kick ass.

Maya Angelou

We have a powerful potential in our youth, and we must have the courage to change old ideas and practices so that we may direct their power toward good ends.

Dr. Mary McLeod Bethune

Look at yourselves. Some of you teen-agers, students. How do you think I feel—and I belong to a generation ahead of you—

how do you think I feel to have to tell you, "We, my generation, sat around like a knot on a wall while the whole world was fighting for its human rights, and you've got to be born into a society where you still have that same fight." What did we do, who preceded you? I'll tell you what we did. Nothing. And don't you make the same mistake we made.

Malcolm X

Mama exhorted her children at every opportunity to "jump at de sun." We might not land on the sun, but at least we would get off the ground.

Zora Neale Hurston

I have faith in young people because I know the strongest emotions which prevail are those of love and caring and belief and tolerance.

Barbara Jordan

I make an active effort to remain a positive role model to kids. They need people to show them there's another way.

M. C. Hammer

My mother could smell whiskey on your breath if she was in the market and you were home in bed.

Eubie Blake

When I used to live in the Brewster projects, I always thought it would be fantastic to have a phone. I would dream about a phone.

Florence Ballard

When you're young, the silliest notions seem the greatest achievements.

Pearl Bailey

The teenagers ain't all bad. I love 'em if nobody else does. There ain't nothin' wrong with young people. Just quit lyin' to 'em.

"Moms" Mabley

Whatever moral qualities I have, come, I'm afraid, from all the sordidness and evil I observed firsthand as a child. However, I do not wish to exaggerate the impact on me of the evil that constantly surrounded me when I was little. I was tough always and, like all slum kids, was able quickly to adjust myself to any and all situations.

God's hand must have closed over me very early in life, making me tough and headstrong and resilient. It is His hand that has carried me safely down the long, dark road I've had to follow since.

Ethel Waters

Seems like God don't see fit to give the black man nothing but dreams—but He did give us children to make them dreams seem worthwhile.

Lorraine Hansberry

Youth is the turning point in life, the most sensitive and volatile period, the state that registers most vividly the impressions and experience of life.

Richard Wright

I would turn in all the Dick Gregorys in the world and all the nightclubs and all the money just to go back to those days [of childhood] and find a daddy there.

Dick Gregory

I wonder how my Momma stayed so good and beautiful in her soul when she worked seven days a week on swollen legs and feet, how she kept teaching us to smile and laugh when the house was dark and cold and she never knew when one of her hungry kids was going to ask about Daddy.

I wonder how she kept from teaching us hate when the social worker came around. She was a nasty bitch with a pinched face who said: "We have reason to suspect you are working, Miss Gregory, and you can be sure I'm going to check on you. We don't stand for welfare cheaters."

Momma, a welfare cheater. A criminal who couldn't stand to see her kids go hungry, or grow up in slums, and end up mugging people in dark corners. I guess the system didn't want her to get off relief, the way it kept sending social workers around to be sure Momma wasn't trying to make things better.

Dick Gregory

When I first became a parent, I had certain ideas about how I was going to control the children, and they all boiled down to this: Children just need love.

Bill Cosby

As anti-white as my father was, he was subconsciously so afflicted with the white man's brainwashing of Negroes that he inclined to favor the light ones and I was his lightest child.

Malcolm X

The number one thing young people in America—indeed young people around the world—have going for them is their sense of honesty, morality, and ethics. Young people refuse to accept the lies and rationalizations of the established order.

Dick Gregory

[My childhood] was lonely. I had one corncob doll, I rode a pig bareback, and spent most of my time reading Bible stories to the barnyard animals. . . . We had an outhouse. You never forget it. No matter how many bathrooms you get, you never forget it.

Oprah Winfrey

If I could change just one thing [in the world], I would stop people from beating their kids. Not just beating, but molesting kids, verbally abusing kids, neglecting kids. The dishonor of children is the single worst problem in this country. If we ended it, there would be an incredible ripple effect on society. From the thousands of shows I've done over the past ten years, I see that the way people were treated as children causes them to grow up and behave in certain ways as adults. I see it as the root of almost every problem in our society.

I think the most important job in the world is raising children. We have seen the toll taken on our children in this generation, and the generation coming, of women and men not being there for their children.

Oprah Winfrey

If we can reach young people's minds deep enough, we can teach young minds deep enough so that they will change the negative concept they have of themselves from which most of the negative social consequences flow.

Ossie Davis

During childhood, I wasn't aware that there was segregation. White people just seemed very alien and strange to me.

Alice Walker

Two parents can't raise a child any more than one. You need a whole community—everybody—to raise a child.

Toni Morrison

Youth are looking for something; it's up to adults to show them what is worth emulating.

Jesse Jackson

The essence of childhood, of course, is play, which my friends and I did endlessly on streets that we reluctantly shared with traffic.

Bill Cosby

I've heard my mother come out of my mouth more often than I ever could have imagined. It wasn't supposed to be that way. I was gonna do it different. I was gonna reason with my kid. I was gonna be down there with her, and know what it was like, and everything would be cool.

Well, please. Kids just don't give a shit. They want what they want when they want it. Period. They don't want to hear your reasoning. They don't want your solidarity. They'll wear you out, just like you wore out your own parents. . . . You'll shake your finger or throw your hands on your hips, same as your mother did, and suddenly you're looking at your own face, and thinking, Oh, shit. Look what I've become—a fax of my folks. An echo.

Whoopi Goldberg

I was twenty-two or twenty-three years old when I did an interview with someone who had been sexually abused [as a child]. It was the first time it occurred to me that this thing that had happened to me had also happened to other people. I hadn't told anybody until then because I thought I was the only person it ever happened to and I thought it was my fault because afterward it happened repeatedly by different people. . . . If you have been sexually abused and kept silent, you keep putting yourself in situations later in life where you can be abused again: by your boss, or by friends who take advantage of you, or by men who say they're going to call, then lie to you, cheat on you. You set yourself up for that. . . . Every bad relationship I've ever been in is the result of my having been abused. . . . What stops this cycle of abuse is awareness.

Oprah Winfrey

One of the things you learn when you become a parent is the horrible thought and the reality that your children will *be* your children for life! That's why there's death.

Bill Cosby

The black youngsters of today must ask black leaders: If you can't make an effort to reach, reconstruct, and save a black man [Clarence Thomas] who has graduated from Yale, how can you reach down here in this drug-filled, hate-filled cesspool where I live and save me?

Maya Angelou

We lived in a number of raggedy houses. The basement of our house was always flooded and I remember we used to have to get in this little boat my brother had gotten for Christmas and paddle over to the washer and dryer to get the clothes in and out.

Terry McMillan

It frightens me that our young black men have a better chance of going to jail than of going to college.

Johnnie Cochran

The civil rights movement didn't really mean much to me as a kid. In New York, it didn't resonate the way it did in the rest of the country. It wasn't about being able to drink from the same fountain or ride the same bus, because we could already do pretty much everything. I could go anywhere. There was no place that was restricted to me. No museum. No store. I could go into Tiffany's if I wanted. That time, to me, was all tied up in Vietnam and the Black Panthers and the Young Lords and the riots at Columbia.

It wasn't until I was an adult that I learned from my mother that her business was more welcome in some stores than in others. She wasn't denied access anywhere, but few department stores would give her a credit card. The first store that ever gave her a credit card was Barneys, on 17th Street, and that's where she dressed my brother, Clyde. She was a loyal customer, especially after she got her credit card, but I liked the jingle for Robert Hall: "When the prices go up, up, up, the value goes down, down, down." Barneys didn't have a jingle, but they gave my mother a credit card.

Whoopi Goldberg

I D E N T I T Y

We ain't what we wanna be, and we ain't what we gonna
be. But thank God, we ain't what we was.

African-American folk saying

For Africa to me . . . is more than a glamorous fact. It is a historical truth. No man can know where he is going unless he
knows exactly where he has been and exactly how he arrived at
his present place.

Maya Angelou

I am born and bred in this America of ours. I want to love it. I
love part of it. But it's up to the rest of America when I shall
love it with the same intensity that I love the Negro people from
whom I sprang.

Paul Robeson

It is a peculiar sensation, this double-consciousness, this sense of always looking at one's self through the eyes of others, of measuring one's soul by the tape of a world that looks on in amused contempt and pity. One ever feels his twoness—an American, a Negro, two souls, two thoughts, two unreconciled strivings; two warring ideals in one dark body.

W.E.B. DuBois

For this, their promise, and for their hard past, I honor the women of my race. Their beauty—their dark and mysterious beauty of midnight eyes, crumpled hair, and soft, full-featured faces—is perhaps more to me than to you, because I was born to its warm and subtle spell; but their worth is yours as well as mine. No other women on earth could have emerged from the hell of force and temptation which once engulfed and still surrounds black women in America with half the modesty and womanliness that they retain. I have always felt like bowing myself before them in all abasement, searching to bring some tribute to these long-suffering victims, these burdened sisters of mine, whom the world, the wise, white world, loves to affront and ridicule and wantonly to insult. I have known the women of many lands and nations—I have known and seen and lived beside them, but none have I known more sweetly feminine, more unswervingly loyal, more desperately earnest, and more instinctively pure in body and in soul than the daughters of my black mothers.

W.E.B. DuBois

I am an African American. I am not ashamed of my African descent. Africa had great universities before there were any in

England and the African was the first man industrious and skill-ful enough to work in iron. If our group must have a special name setting it apart, the sensible way to settle it would be to refer to our ancestors, the Africans, from whom our swarthy complexions come.

Mary Church Terrell

The majority of [the black bourgeoisie] go through life denounc-ing white people because they are trying to run away from blacks and decrying the blacks because they are not white.

Carter G. Woodson

None of us is responsible for the complexion of his skin. This fact of nature offers no clue to the character or quality of the person underneath.

Marian Anderson

We're not Americans, we're Africans who happen to be in Amer-ica. We were kidnapped and brought here against our will from Africa. We didn't land on Plymouth Rock—that rock landed on us.

Malcolm X

My fondest hope is that *Roots* may start black, white, brown, red, yellow people digging back for their own roots. Man, that would make me feel 90 feet tall.

Alex Haley

Your own need to be shines out of any dream or creation you imagine.

James Earl Jones

If you are going to think black, think positive about it. Don't think down on it, or think it is something in your way. And this way, when you really do want to stretch out, and express how beautiful black is, everybody will hear you.

Leontyne Price

There is definitely a burden to carry [in creating role models], but I think that responsibility has always made blacks that choose to carry the burden stronger. Jackie Robinson, being the first black ever to play major-league baseball, he wasn't just a ballplayer. He had to be extra special. That's something to deal with, but it's almost a good thing. It makes you work harder. I want to play positive characters. I want to play characters that represent really strong, positive black images. So that's the thing I consider when I'm taking a role after I decide if it's something that I want to do. At this point, I don't want to play a gangster, unless it's a role that has a different or more positive message. It's a large part of why I don't rap now, because of the slant that rap music has taken.

Will Smith

An identity would seem to be arrived at by the way in which the person faces and uses his experience.

James Baldwin

There can be no greater tragedy than to forget one's origin and finish despised and hated by the people among whom one grew up. To have that happen would be the sort of thing to make me rise up from my grave.

Paul Robeson

To me, the black black woman is our essential mother—the blacker she is the more us she is—and to see the hatred that is turned on her is enough to make me despair, almost entirely, of our future as a people.

Alice Walker

Be not deceived,
The struggle is far from over,
The best of being Black is yet to be—
So said the Ones who Died to set you free.

Ossie Davis

Eddie [Murphy] is the only person that I ever imitated. It's like, with my friends, Eddie inspired a generation of black comedians, in the same way that Richard Pryor inspired the generation after him. In our lives, we have things that we say that are Eddie Murphy lines from movies. . . . We've created a dialogue that Eddie Murphy supplies. He's the person that made me see that, okay, maybe I can do this. Because I had never even thought about acting, but seeing Eddie, and being able to be in the mirror delivering Eddie Murphy lines the way that he delivers them, made me feel that I could do it.

Will Smith

It no longer bothers me that I may be constantly searching for father figures; by this time, I have found several and dearly enjoyed knowing them all.

Alice Walker

When you're called a nigger you look at your father because you think your father can rule the world—every kid thinks that—and then you discover that your father cannot do anything about it. So you begin to despise your father and you realize, oh, that's what a nigger is.

James Baldwin

The fact that the adult American Negro female emerges a formidable character is often met with amazement, distaste and even belligerence. It is seldom accepted as an inevitable outcome of the struggle won by survivors, and deserves respect if not enthusiastic acceptance.

Maya Angelou

There are those who believe black people possess the secret of joy and that it is this that will sustain them through any spiritual or moral or physical devastation.

Alice Walker

The emotional, sexual, and psychological stereotyping of females begins when the doctor says: "It's a girl."

Shirley Chisholm

I had gone to Europe . . . to reach for a place as a serious artist, but I never doubted that I must return. I was—and am—an American.

Marian Anderson

Black is beautiful when it is a slum kid studying to enter college, when it is a man learning new skills for a new job.

Whitney M. Young, Jr.

I am the product of hatred and love—the hatred of the social and political structure which dominated the segregated, hate-filled city of my youth, and the love of some people—my mother, my grandparents, my neighbors and relatives—who said by their actions, "You can make it, but first you must endure."

Clarence Thomas

All of us are black first, and everything else second.

Malcolm X

We allow our ignorance to prevail upon us and make us think we can survive alone, alone in patches, alone in groups, alone in races, even alone in genders.

Maya Angelou

One of the things that made the Black Muslim movement grow was its emphasis upon things African. This was the secret to the growth of the Black Muslim movement. African blood, Af-

rican origin, African culture, African ties. And you'd be surprised—we discovered that deep within the subconscious of the
black man in this country, he is still more African than he is
American.

Malcolm X

Where can we find in this race of ours real men? Men of character, men of purpose, men of confidence, men of faith, men
who really know themselves? I have come across so many weak-
lings who profess to be leaders, and in the test I have found
them but the slaves to a nobler class. They perform the will of
their masters without question.

Marcus Garvey

I'm the man you think you are. . . . If you want to know what
I'll do, figure out what you'll do. I'll do the same thing—only
more of it.

Malcolm X

Any strategy for dealing with the contemporary crisis in black
America should be based on a principle that respects black
America's moral identity and heritage. Given what we have
learned of the black-American strategy for survival during and
in the aftermath of slavery, that principle may be summarized
as the primacy of moral/spiritual over material values; and
therefore, the primacy of organic institutions (e.g., family,
church, neighborhood) over inorganic institutions (e.g., money,
government, bureaucracy).

Alan Keyes

Bureaucracies are inherently antidemocratic. Bureaucrats derive their power from their position in the structure, not from their relations with the people they are supposed to serve. The people are not masters of the bureaucracy, but its clients. They receive its services, but only insofar as they conform to its authority. The bureaucracy is like a computer; it responds only to those who address it in the proper form. In this sense, a bureaucratic government program has a double meaning: The program serves its clients, but it also programs them.

Alan Keyes

It's just like when you've got some coffee that's too black, which means it's too strong. What do you do? You integrate it with cream, you make it weak. But if you pour too much cream in it, you won't even know you ever had coffee. It used to be hot, it becomes cool. It used to be strong, it becomes weak. It used to wake you up, now it puts you to sleep.

Malcolm X

Sitting at the table doesn't make you a diner. You must be eating some of what's on that plate. Being here in America doesn't make you an American. Being born here in America doesn't make you an American.

Therefore, we pledge to bind ourselves again to one another;
To embrace our lowliest,
To keep company with our loneliest,
To educate our illiterate,
To feed our starving,
To clothe our ragged,

To do all good things, knowing that we are more than keepers
of our brothers and sisters. We are our brothers and sisters.
In honor of those who toiled and implored God with golden
tongues, and in gratitude to the same God who brought us
out of hopeless desolation,
We make this pledge.

Maya Angelou

We younger Negro artists now intend to express our individual
dark-skinned selves without fear or shame. If white people are
pleased, we are glad. If they aren't, it doesn't matter. We know
we are beautiful. And ugly too . . . If colored people are pleased,
we are glad. If they are not, their displeasure doesn't matter
either. We build our temples for tomorrow, as strong as we know
how, and we stand on the top of the mountain, free within
ourselves.

Langston Hughes

To me, a man has no master but God. Man in his authority is
a sovereign lord. As for the individual man, so of the individual
race. This feeling makes man so courageous, so bold, as to make
it impossible for his brother to intrude upon his rights. So few
of us can understand what it takes to make a man—the man
who will never say die; the man who will never give up; the man
who will never depend upon others to do for him what he ought
to do for himself; the man who will not blame God, who will
not blame Nature, will not blame Fate for his condition; but the
man who will go out and make conditions to suit himself. Oh,
how disgusting life becomes when on every hand you hear peo-

ple (who bear your image, who bear your resemblance) telling you that they cannot make it, that Fate is against them, that they cannot get a chance. If 400,000,000 Negroes can only get to know themselves, to know that in them is a sovereign power, is an authority that is absolute, then in the next twenty-four hours we would have a new race, we would have a nation, an empire, resurrected not from the will of others to see us rise, but from our own determination to rise, irrespective of what the world thinks.

Marcus Garvey

The black kids, the poor white kids, Spanish-speaking kids, and Asian kids in the U.S.—in the face of everything to the contrary, they still bop and bump, shout and go to school somehow. Their optimism gives me hope.

Maya Angelou

When I discover who I am, I'll be free.

Ralph Ellison

Those are the same stars, and that is the same moon, that look down upon your brothers and sisters, and which they see as they look up to them, though they are ever so far away from us, and each other.

Sojourner Truth

Character, not circumstances, makes the man.

Booker T. Washington

Ain't no man can avoid being born average, but there ain't no man got to be common.

Satchel Paige

For I am my mother's daughter, and the drums of Africa still beat in my heart. They will not let me rest while there is still a single Negro boy or girl without a chance to prove his worth.

Mary McLeod Bethune

Please stop using the word Negro. We are the only human beings in the world with fifty-seven varieties of complexions who are classed together in a single racial unit. Therefore, we are really colored people and that is the only name in the English language which accurately describes us.

Mary Church Terrell (Washington Post, *1949*)

It is not skin color which makes a Negro American, but cultural heritage as shaped by the American experience, the social and political predicament.

Ralph Ellison

Despite the terrorization which the Negro in America endured and endures sporadically until today, despite the cruel and totally inescapable ambivalence of his status in this country, the battle for his identity has long ago been won. He is not a visitor to the West, but a citizen there, an American.

James Baldwin

Advice to Negro writers: Step *outside yourself*, then look back—
and you will see how human, yet how beautiful and black you
are. How very black—even when you're integrated.

Langston Hughes

I'm not a Negro tennis player. I'm a tennis player.

Althea Gibson

I've always had confidence. It came because I have lots of initiative. I wanted to make something of myself.

Eddie Murphy

Will somebody please tell me what Althea Gibson is if she is
not a Negro tennis player? Did the Negroes who housed, fed,
clothed, and educated her, free of charge, do so because she
was a tennis player or because she is a Negro tennis player? Did
the American Tennis Association fight for her to get a chance
to play in the big national tournaments because she was a tennis
player or because she is a Negro tennis player?

P. L. Prattis (Pittsburgh Courier, *1959*)

You know why Madison Avenue advertising has never done well
in Harlem? We're the only ones who know what it means to be
brand X.

Dick Gregory

A man without knowledge of himself and his heritage is like a tree without roots.

Dick Gregory

We live surrounded by white images, and white in this world is synonymous with the good, light, beauty, success, so that, despite ourselves sometimes, we run after that whiteness and deny our darkness, which has been made into the symbol of all that is evil or inferior.

Paule Marshall

Sociologists often assert that there is a Negro thing—a timbre of voice, a style, a rhythm—in all of its positive and negative implications, the expression of a certain kind of American uniqueness. If there is this uniqueness, why on earth would it not in some way be precious to the people who maintain it?

Ralph Ellison

The Negro's relationship with one another is utterly deplorable. The Negro wants to be everything but himself. He wants to be a white man. He processes his hair. Acts like a white man. He wants to integrate with the white man, but he cannot integrate with himself or with his own kind. The Negro wants to lose his identity because he does not know his identity.

Elijah Muhammad

In [Marcus] Garvey's time, the "Back to Africa" movement had an appeal and probably made some sense. But it doesn't make any sense now, because the black people of America aren't Africans any more, and the Africans don't want them.

Chester Himes

The position of the Negro in American culture is indeed a paradox. It almost passes understanding how and why a group of people who can be socially despised, yet at the same time artistically esteemed and culturally influential, can be both an oppressed minority and a dominant cultural force.

Alain Locke

The Black man must find himself as a Black man before he can find himself as an American. He must now become a hyphenated American discovering the hyphen so he can eventually lose it.

James Farmer

I find, in being black, a thing of beauty: a joy, a strength; a secret cup of gladness—a native land in neither time nor place—a native land in every Negro face! Be loyal to yourselves: your skin, your hair, your lips, your southern speech, your laughing kindness—are Negro kingdoms, vast as any other.

Ossie Davis

For it means something to be a Negro, after all, as it means something to have been born in Ireland or in China, to live where one sees space and sky or to live where one sees nothing but rubble or nothing but high buildings.

James Baldwin

We must recapture our heritage and our ideals if we are to liberate ourselves from the bonds of white supremacy. We must launch a cultural revolution to unbrainwash an entire people.

Malcolm X

The American image of the Negro lives also in the Negro's heart; and when he has surrendered to this image, life has no other possible reality.

James Baldwin

Many people will teach you that the Black man in this country doesn't identify with Africa. Before 1959, many Negroes didn't. But before 1959, the image of Africa was created by an enemy of Africa, because Africans weren't in a position to create and project their own images. Such an image of the Africans was so hateful to Afro-Americans that they refused to identify with Africa. We did not realize that in hating Africa and the Africans, we were hating ourselves. You cannot hate the roots of a tree and not hate the tree itself.

Malcolm X

I suppose that regardless of what any Negro in America might do or how high he might rise in social status, he still has something in common with every other Negro.

Claude Brown

We're a great heart people.

Pearl Bailey

To be a Negro in America is to hope against hope.

Martin Luther King, Jr.

I love America more than any other country in the world, and, exactly for this reason, I insist on the right to criticize her perpetually.

James Baldwin

The black's whole image is changing. He's no longer being thought of as shiftless, lazy; now he's thought of as a tough son of a bitch.

Bill Cosby

There's a period of life when we swallow a knowledge of ourselves and it becomes either good or sour inside.

Pearl Bailey

It isn't a matter of black is beautiful as much as it is white is not *all* that's beautiful.

Bill Cosby

I hear that melting-pot stuff a lot, and all I can say is that we haven't melted.

Jesse Jackson

Black people cannot and will not become integrated into American society on any terms but those of self-determination and autonomy.

Gerda Lerner

A word to the wise ain't necessary—it's the stupid ones who need advice.

Bill Cosby

Every generation needs the instruction and insights of past generations in order to forge its own vision.

Jesse Jackson

Every man is born into the world to do something unique and something distinctive, and if he or she does not do it, it will never be done.

Dr. Benjamin E. Mays

Can't nothing make your life work if you ain't the architect.

Terry McMillan

During those days [the 1950s], no one in America was closer to the pulse of colored life than the society editors of the black press. Through their columns and news items about the most intimate phases of black life, they did more to interpret the social patterns of the community than the sociologists or psychologists.

Geraldyn Hodges Major

The challenge facing us is to equip ourselves that we will be able to take our place wherever we are in the affairs of men.

Barbara Jordan

We really are fifteen countries and it's really remarkable that each of us thinks we represent the real America. The Midwesterner in Kansas, the black American in Durham—both are certain they are the real American.

Maya Angelou

America is me. It gave me the only life I know, so I must share in its survival.

Gordon Parks

I make bold to assert that it took more courage for Martin Luther King, Jr., to practice nonviolence than it took his assassin to fire the fatal shot.

Dr. Benjamin E. Mays

If Rosa Parks had not refused to move to the back of the bus, you and I might never have heard of Dr. Martin Luther King.

Ramsey Clark

I used to be very hurt [when people called me an "Oreo"], and I used to always think I had to defend it and always make people know that yes, I really am black and I really am proud of it, and no, I'm not an Oreo at all. I don't feel that anymore because I know in my spirit that I care about what happens to black people and people in this country.

Oprah Winfrey

When people watch television, they are looking to see themselves. I think the reason why I work so well as I do on the air is the people sense the *realness*. . . . My greatest gift is my ability to be myself at all times, no matter what. I am as comfortable in front of the camera with a million people watching me as I am sitting here talking to you.

Oprah Winfrey

When I first told my wife I was thinking about observing Kwanzaa, she barred the way to our attic and said she'd never chuck our Christmas tree lights and antique ornaments. I told her that wouldn't be necessary. Kwanzaa does not replace Christmas and is not a religious holiday. It is a time to focus on Africa and African-inspired culture and to reinforce a value system that goes back for generations.

Eric V. Copage

There are still a lot of black people who are very angry and bitter. They want me to be just as angry and bitter, and I won't be. It just burns me. Some black people say I'm not black enough. I wonder, how black do you have to be? The drums of Africa still beat in my heart, and they will not rest until every black boy and every black girl has had a chance to prove their worth.

Oprah Winfrey

I am proud to be a black American.

Michael Jackson

Over the years, myriad surgeries have changed his features and left me confused about who [Michael Jackson] is and who he aspires to be. And I'm sorry, but after all the caucasianizing cuts, I question Michael's explanation that some rare pigment affliction is the reason his skin is so pale.

Pamela Johnson

I am where I am because of the bridges that I crossed. Sojourner Truth was a bridge. Harriet Tubman was a bridge. Ida B. Wells was a bridge. Madame C. J. Walker was a bridge. Fannie Lou Hamer was a bridge.

Oprah Winfrey

I'm setting up trust funds for [my sons] to go to the best colleges my money can pay for. I would rather see them as young, smart, black businessmen than as athletes because everybody knows what a black athlete is.

Bo Jackson

This idea of identity through genetic accident and ethnic costumes dominated by Kente cloth motifs is both misbegotten and fruitless.

Stanley Crouch

I am very much aware of my black heritage, but I'm also aware of the other elements of who I am. And I think sometimes it bothers people [who would prefer me to say] that I'm black and that's it. . . . When people ask, I say I'm black, Venezuelan, and Irish because that's who I am.

Mariah Carey

Call me an asshole, call me a blowhard, but don't call me an African American. Please. It divides us, as a nation and as a people, and it kinda pisses me off. It diminishes everything I've accomplished and everything every other black person has accomplished on American soil. It means I'm not entitled to everything plain old regular Americans are entitled to.

Every time you put something in front of the word *American*, it strips it of its meaning. The Bill of Rights is my Bill of Rights, same as anyone else's. It's my flag. It's my Constitution. It doesn't talk about *some* people. It talks about *all* people—black, white, orange, brown. You. Me. . . .

Black people, stop trying to identify elsewhere. This is yours. People in the South got their legs chewed off, got hit with fire hoses, got their children blown up, got yanked, burned, hanged, and sliced so that you wouldn't have to pretend you were from someplace else. So that you wouldn't have to say, "No, I'm not entitled to this." Well, fuck that. You're entitled to all of it. Take it. It's ours.

Whoopi Goldberg

Nature created no races.

John Henrik Clarke

As early as 1901, West Indians owned 20 percent of all black businesses in Manhattan, although they were only 10 percent of the black population there.

Thomas Sowell

Would America have been America without her Negro people?

W.E.B. DuBois

I was thinking about all the honors that are showered on me in the theater, how everyone wishes to shake my hand or get an autograph, a real hero, you'd naturally think. However, when I reach a hotel, I am refused permission to ride on the passenger elevator, I cannot enter the dining room for my meals, and am Jim Crowed generally. I know this to be an unbelievable custom.

Bert Williams

Those who become inoculated with the virus of race hatred are more unfortunate than the victims of it. Race hatred is the most malignant poison that can afflict the mind. It freezes up the fount of inspiration and chills the higher faculties of the soul.

Kelly Miller

[White] southerners are not two-faced. If they don't like you, they'll let you know it, but if they love you, they'll die for you. They won't do like some folks I know up the [North] country, smile in your face, pat you on the shoulder, then knife you in the back first chance they get.

Bill "Bojangles" Robinson

America is woven of many strands; I would recognize them and let it so remain. . . . Our fate is to become one, and yet many. This is not prophecy, but description.

Ralph Ellison

Men must be carefully taught to hate, and the lessons learned by one generation must be relearned by the next.

Lerone Bennett, Jr.

The white man knows what a revolution is. He knows that the Black Revolution is worldwide in scope and in nature. The Black Revolution is sweeping Asia, is sweeping Africa, is rearing its head in Latin America. The Cuban Revolution—that's a revolution. They overturned the system. Revolution is in Asia, revolution is in Africa, and the white man is screaming because he sees revolution in Latin America. How do you think he'll react to you when you learn what a real revolution is?

Malcolm X

One thing is clear to me: We, as human beings, must be willing to accept people who are different from ourselves.

Barbara Jordan

I think there is racism in every aspect of American culture and life, so why would we think it would be any different [in Hollywood]? It's a part of living in our world and it's something that, unfortunately, we all have to deal with. I think it's a cancer that erodes the very base of our existence.

Will Smith

Even those things that were possible [in Hollywood] 50 years ago were not done. . . . There were people of quite extraordinary gifts—educators and business people—all within the structure of a segregated society, but the [movie] industry had no need, no compunction to treat the black community other than how they perceived them.

Sidney Poitier

The trouble with our people is as soon as they got out of slavery they didn't want to give the white man nothing else. But the fact is, you got to give 'em something. Either your money, your land, your woman, or your ass.

Alice Walker

I had a power, and the power that I had—the only power that I had—was to say no. I had no power to influence, I had no power to instruct. I only had the power to say no. And that was sufficient, for me. I said, "No, I don't want to do that. No, I cannot do that. No, I'm not available for that."

Sidney Poitier (discussing the peak of his career in the mid-1960s)

Who ever heard of angry revolutionists all harmonizing "We shall overcome . . . Suum Day . . ." while tripping and swaying along arm-in-arm with the very people they were supposed to be angrily revolting against? Who ever heard of angry revolutionists swinging their bare feet together with their oppressor in lily-pad park pools, with gospels and guitars and "I have a dream" speeches? And the black masses in America were—and still are—having a nightmare.

Malcolm X

America's mission was and still is to take diversity and mold it into a cohesive and coherent whole that would espouse virtues and values essential to the maintenance of civil order. There is nothing easy about that mission. But it is not mission impossible.

Barbara Jordan

I'm not a separatist. The imagination is integrative. That's how you make the new—by putting something else with what you've got. And I'm unashamedly an American integrationist.

Ralph Ellison

It is up to us in the north to provide aid and support to those who are actually bearing the brunt of the fight for equality down south. America has its iron curtain too.

Jackie Robinson

I'm pleased God made my skin black; I wish He'd made it thicker.

Curt Flood

To tolerate anti-Semitism is to cooperate with the evils of prejudice and bigotry that Martin Luther King, Jr., fought against. In a speech he delivered one month before he was assassinated, my husband said, "For the black man to struggle for justice and then turn around and be anti-Semitic is not only a very irrational course, but it is a very immoral course, and wherever we have seen anti-Semitism we have condemned it with all our might."

Coretta Scott King (when she was asked how her husband would have responded to the anti-Jewish sentiments expressed by African-American leaders like Louis Farrakhan and Al Sharpton)

We learn about one another's culture the same way we learn about sex: in the streets.

Ishmael Reed

I have come to believe two things that might seem contradictory: Some of our worst childhood fears were true—the establishment is teeming with racism. Yet I also believe whites are as befuddled about race as we are, and they're as scared of us as we are of them. Many of them are seeking solutions, just like us.

Nathan McCall

As far as I knew, white women were never lonely, except in books. White men adored them, Black men desired them and Black women worked for them.

Maya Angelou

Once you begin to explain or excuse all events on racial grounds, you begin to indulge in the perilous mythology of race.

James Earl Jones

Our too-young and too-new America, lusty because it is lonely, aggressive because it is afraid, insists upon seeing the world in terms of good and bad, the holy and the evil, the high and the low, the white and the black; our America is frightened of fact, of history, of processes, of necessity. It hugs the easy way of damning those whom it cannot understand, of excluding those whom it cannot understand, of excluding those who look different, and it salves its conscience with a self-draped cloak of righteousness.

Richard Wright

How did I deal with racism? I beat it. I said, "I am not going to carry this burden of racism. I'm going to destroy your stereotype. I'm proud to be black. You carry this burden of racism, because I'm not going to."

Colin Powell

Prejudice is like a hair across your cheek. You can't see it, you can't find it with your fingers, but you keep brushing at it because the feel of it is irritating.

Marian Anderson

Fairness is an across-the-board requirement for all our interactions with each other . . . . Fairness treats everybody the same.

Barbara Jordan

[Martin Luther King, Jr.] got the peace prize, we got the problem. . . . If I'm following a general, and he's leading me into a battle, and the enemy tends to give him rewards, or awards, I get suspicious of him. Especially if he gets a peace award before the war is over.

Malcolm X

The white man is always trying to nose into somebody else's business. All right, I'll set something outside the door of my mind for him to play with and handle. He can read my writing, but he sho' can't read my mind. Then I'll say my say and sing my song.

Zora Neale Hurston

I had a hard lesson to learn, that I could not help others free their hearts and minds of racial prejudice unless I would do all I could within myself to straighten out my own thinking and to feel and respond to kindness, to goodwill from wherever it came, whether it was the southerner, northerner, or any race.

Rosa Parks

The only way to get equality is for two people to get the same thing at the same time at the same place.

Thurgood Marshall

I got the feeling on hearing the discussion yesterday that when you put a white child in school with a whole lot of colored children, the child would fall apart or something. Now is the time for this Court to make clear that is not what our Constitution stands for.

Thurgood Marshall

Among the women of the black bourgeoisie there is an intense fear of the competition of white women for the Negro men. They often attempt to rationalize their fear by saying that the Negro man always occupies an inferior position in relation to the white woman or that he marries much below his "social" status. They come nearer to the source of their fear when they confess that there are not many eligible Negro men and that these few should marry Negro women. That such rationalizations conceal deep-seated feelings of insecurity is revealed by the fact that generally they have no objection to the marriage of white men to Negro women, especially if the white man is reputed to be wealthy. In fact, they take pride in the fact and attribute these marriages to the "peculiar" charms of Negro women. In fact, the middle-class Negro woman's fear of the competition of white women is based often upon the fact that she senses her own inadequacies and shortcomings. Her position in Negro "society" and in the larger Negro community is often due to some adventitious factor, such as a light complexion or a meager education, which has pushed her to the top of the social pyramid. The middle-class white woman not only has a white skin and straight hair, but she is generally more sophisticated and interesting because she has read more widely and has a larger view of the world. The middle-class Negro woman may make fun of the "plainness" of her white competitor and the latter's lack of "wealth" and interest in "society"; nevertheless, she still feels insecure when white women appear as even potential competitors.

E. Franklin Frazier

I would like to point something out so that we'll understand each other better. I don't want you to think in the statements I made that I'm being disrespectful towards you as white people. I'm being frank. And I think that my statements will give you a better insight on the mind of a black man than most statements you get from most people who call themselves Negroes, who usually tell you what they want you to hear with the hope . . . that will make them draw closer to you and create a better possibility of getting from you some of the crumbs that you might let fall from your table. Well, I'm not looking for crumbs, so I'm not trying to delude you.

Malcolm X

I came from what was called one of the First Families of Brook-lyn. It was a family that never talked about the fact that we were all the descendants of slave women. Yet it was the rape of slave women by their masters which accounted for our white blood, which, in turn, made us Negro "society." I realize now, that as a child and young girl, I did not know who I was or what I was—because nobody ever told me. . . . I certainly never learned anything about my identity in school, because the only Negro mentioned in history books was George Washington Carver, and he was too pure and good to believe, though I did learn that other races had backgrounds they looked upon with pride. I kept trying to find some reason to feel the same way.

Lena Horne

In Dixie there are two worlds, the white world and the black world, and they are physically separated. There are white schools and black schools, white churches and black churches, white businesses and black businesses, white graveyards and black graveyards, and, for all I know, a white God and a black God.

Richard Wright

Many interviewers when they come to talk to me, think they're being progressive by not mentioning in their stories any longer that I'm black. I tell them, "Don't stop now. If I shot somebody you'd mention it."

Colin Powell

We can go on talking about racism and who treated whom badly, but what are you going to do about it? Are you going to wallow in that or are you going to create your own agenda?

Judith Jamison

You lose a lot of time, hating people.

Marian Anderson

Being black in America has nothing to do with skin color. To be black means that your soul, your mind, and your body are where the dispossessed are.

James Cone

I have been asked by people who obviously don't know me very well how I feel when I look at television and see white policemen knocking down Negro women with fire hoses and then look at my husband and know that he is white. This kind of question is just as stupid and unfortunately just as normal as the people who make it. Don't they understand that when you look at people you love—husband or friend—you don't see *color*? It so happens that Lennie is the kindest person I have ever known. And I know that his reaction to savagery is just as strong, if not stronger, than my own. I say that his reaction might be stronger because he is perhaps less used to it than I am.

Lena Horne

I just want to know how come Adam and Eve was white. If they had started out black, this world might not be in the fix it is today. Eve might not have paid that serpent no attention. I never did know a Negro yet that liked a snake.

Langston Hughes

Anything that is as old as racism is in the blood line of the nation. It's not any superficial thing—that attitude is in the blood and we have to educate it out.

Nannie Burroughs

You gotta realize, my people have never known what job security is. For instance, come another recession and the economy has to tighten its belt—who do you think's gonna be the first notch?

Dick Gregory

Many of our white brothers fail to interpret correctly the nature of the Negro Revolution. Some believe that it is the work of skilled agitators who have the power to raise or lower the floodgates at will.

Martin Luther King, Jr.

Racism seems ageless—like the passion of those who war against it.

Gordon Parks

Our real victory is not so much the desegregation of the buses as it is a new sense of dignity and destiny.

Martin Luther King, Jr.

One Negro mother put rather well the feelings I have heard many others express: "I guess we all don't like white people too much deep inside. You could hardly expect us to, after what's happened all these years. It's in our bones to be afraid of them, and bones have a way of staying around even when everything else is gone. But if something is inside of you, it doesn't mean it's there alone. We have to live with one another, black with white, I mean. I keep on telling that to the children, and if they don't seem to learn it, like everything else, I have to punish them to make sure they do. . . . Just the other day my Laura started getting sassy about white children on the television. My husband told her to hold her tongue and do it fast. It's like with cars and knives, you have to teach your children what's dangerous and how to stay away from it, or else they won't live long. White people are a real danger to us until we learn how to live with them. So if you want your kids to live long, they have to grow up scared of whites; and the way they get scared is through us; and that's why I don't let my kids get fresh about the white man even in their own house. If I do, there's liable to be trouble to pay. They'll forget, and they'll say something outside, and that'll be it for them, and us too. So I make them store it in their bones, way inside, and then no one sees it. Maybe in a joke we'll have once in a while, or something like that, you can see what we feel inside, but mostly it's buried. . . . The colored man, I think he has to hide what he really feels even from himself. Otherwise, there would be too much pain—too much."

Robert Coles

When I say the white man is a devil, I speak with the authority of history.

Malcolm X

In the context of the Negro problem, neither whites nor blacks, for excellent reasons of their own, have the faintest desire to look back; but I think that the past is all that makes the present coherent, and further, that the past will remain horrible for exactly as long as we refuse to assess it honestly.

James Baldwin

Men often hate each other because they fear each other; they fear each other because they do not know each other; they do not know each other because they cannot communicate; they cannot communicate because they are separated.

A. Philip Randolph

Protest literature is finally a plea to white America for our human dignity. We cannot get it that way. We must address each other's beauty, wonder, and pain.

Laurence P. Neal

Since the earliest days of this nation's history, students attending its schools have achieved competence in the four, not three, "Rs": Reading Riting, Rithmetic, and Racism.

Malcolm X

Racism is a scholarly pursuit; it's taught, it's institutionalized.

Toni Morrison

Just being a Negro doesn't qualify you to understand the race situation any more than being sick makes you an expert on medicine.

Dick Gregory

If we—and I mean the relatively conscious whites and the relatively conscious blacks, who must, like lovers, insist on, or create the consciousness of others—do not falter in our duty now, we may be able, handful that we are, to end the racial nightmare of our country and change the history of the world.

James Baldwin

I am not anti-American. I think there are plenty of good people in America, but there are also plenty of bad people in America—and the bad ones are the ones that seem to have all the power.

Malcolm X

There is, I should think, no Negro living in America who has not felt, briefly or for long periods, with anguish sharp or dull, in varying degrees and to varying effect, simple, naked, and unanswerable hatred.

James Baldwin

You gotta say this for whites, their self-confidence knows no bounds. Who else could go to a small island in the South Pacific, where there's no crime, poverty, unemployment, war, or worry—and call it a primitive society.

Dick Gregory

It is quite possible to say that the price a Negro pays for becoming articulate is to find himself, at length, with nothing to be articulate about.

James Baldwin

Most whites, even when they credit a Negro with some intelligence, will still feel that all he can talk about is the race issue. . . . Just notice how rarely you will hear whites asking any Negroes what they think about the problem of the world health or the space race to land men on the moon.

Malcolm X

America needs to understand Islam, because this is the one religion that erases from its society the race problem. Throughout my travels in the Muslim world, I have met, talked to, and even eaten with people who in America would have been considered "white"—but the "white" attitude was removed from their minds by the religion of Islam. I have never before seen *sincere* and *true* brotherhood practiced by all colors together, irrespective of their color.

Malcolm X

If a man like Malcolm X could change and repudiate racism, if I myself and other former Muslims can change, if young whites can change, then there is hope for America.

Eldridge Cleaver

Racism is so universal in this country, so widespread, and deep-seated, that it is invisible because it is so normal.

Shirley Chisholm

Discrimination and intolerance will eat you up and destroy whatever creativity was in you if you let it.

Gordon Parks

I believe racism has killed more people than speed, heroin, or cancer, and will continue to kill until it is no more.

Alice Childress

The price of hating other human beings is loving oneself less.

Eldridge Cleaver

Most Negroes have a little black militancy swimming around in them and most white people have a little Ku Klux Klan swimming around in them. If we'd be honest with each other, we would discover we are all victims of the racism that is historically part of this country.

Barbara Jordan

It must be remembered that during most of the past 200 years, the Constitution, as interpreted by this Court, did not prohibit the most ingenious and pervasive forms of discrimination against the Negro. Now, when a Senate acts to remedy the effects of that legacy of discrimination, I cannot believe that this same Constitution stands as a barrier.

Thurgood Marshall

Black people are the people who fight wars for this country against other people of color around the world. Recent examples are Vietnam and Grenada.

Haki R. Madhubuti

Our flag is red, white, and blue, but our nation is rainbow—red, yellow, brown, black, and white—we're all precious in God's sight. America is not like a blanket—one piece of unbroken cloth, the same color, the same texture, the same size. America is more like a quilt—many patches, many pieces, many colors, many sizes, all woven and held together by a common thread.

Jesse Jackson

You learn about equality in history and civics, but you find out life is not really like that.

Arthur Ashe

They ought to pick more fair-minded people to be police officers, because the job's too important to have any kind of racist white person walking around with a gun and a license to kill.

Miles Davis

I am strained to defend racial quotas and any affirmative action that supersedes merit. And I believe there was much that Reagan had to offer blacks.

Shelby Steele

A white child might need a role model, but a black child needs more than that in this society. He needs hope.

Hank Aaron

White Anglo-Saxon males never have felt inferior as a result of their centuries of "affirmative action" and quotas . . . in jobs from which Jews, racial minorities, and women were excluded and too often still are.

Marian Wright Edelman

With more blacks and other people of color, there will be a tilt in power, and whites will be in the minority. It is in the best interests of white people to work harder to create better relationships with people of color so they can ensure themselves the equality that has eluded us.

Representative Maxine Waters

There's a subconscious racism that's been driven on blacks so hard that it's become part of their attitude about everything. But you cannot become part of the oppression. I want to hear black people say, "I can do anything!" I'm not one of those guys who uses the word "nigger" for fun. And I don't use it onstage to entertain. Never.

I am angry. I'm on a tightrope, and people are punching me from every direction. I give 110 percent. I resent the fact that for some white critics I have to be whiter to be a star. And then there are jabs from my own people, the implication that I have to be unfair to whites to make blacks happy.

Arsenio Hall

I plan to be a major player in the entertainment industry. It's about time there was a black man who doesn't have to give up his blackness in order to play with the white guys.

Russell Simmons

I can satisfy every group and get canceled and not satisfy anybody. . . . I had a woman tell me the other day I don't have enough pretty black women on the show. You have no idea how I break my ass to give people what they want. . . .

You'd be surprised how many people come to the show and say, 'I don't know if Arsenio is aware of . . . but would you please not get into it?' Please don't fault me because the people who come on my show don't choose to talk about their sexual preferences.

I don't do [Andrew] Dice Clay–type jokes about gay people. I believe if my gay friends come on the show, I don't have to take them out [of the closet]. I hear gay jokes that, as a heterosexual man, bother me. I've heard jokes that could make a man go out and punch somebody in the face, and that bothers me. I don't think I'm a bad guy—if I were, my gay friends would tell me. . . .

The thing that amazes me is that Johnny Carson just did thirty years [as a talk-show host]. Have I done less than him in bringing these people to the air? I've never seen Queer Nation jump up at Johnny Carson. Sometimes I watch my show and say, 'Johnny never had to do this.' They'd never do that to a white man. They've never done it to Johnny; they've never done it to David Letterman. I probably have the largest gay and female staff in this town, and you've got an organization coming to me and saying I'm prejudiced. Bullshit! I have respect for the struggle of the Queer Nation, but please don't end my career with your struggle.

> *Arsenio Hall (responding to accusations of homophobia*
> *from a radical gay organization that also called for a boy-*
> *cott of his television show)*

When you're black, being invisible to whites is a way of life. Most white people look right through black people as if they aren't there.

Darryl Strawberry

I'm tired of *Miss Daisy*. I am tired of books and movies and plays written by white folks about the good old days when servants were patient, loyal, long-suffering, and black.

Pearl Cleage

Once you begin to explain or excuse all events on racial grounds, you begin to indulge in the perilous mythology of race. It is dangerous to say, "The white man is the cause of my problems," or, "The black man is the cause of my problems." Substitute any color—the danger is implicit.

James Earl Jones

White women have benefited the most from affirmative action.

Anita Doreen Diggs

If [white journalist] Pete Hamill thinks it's a good idea for black middle-class people to return to the ghettoes to aid their underclass brothers and sisters, then why isn't it a good idea for Mr. Hamill to relocate to South Boston or the Bronx to aid the Irish-American underclass?

Ishmael Reed

In recent issues of popular black magazines, black writers have gone through lengthy gyrations trying to justify using the "N" word. . . . They missed the point. Words are not value neutral. . . . They reflect society's standards. The word "nigger" does precisely that; it is the most hurtful and enduring symbol of black oppression.

Earl Ofari Hutchinson

The war on drugs has become a war on the minority community.

Reverend Leonard B. Jackson

Reconciliation and healing are the prescription for America's intractable race problem. But healing is made difficult by our inability to put events and feelings in a timely perspective. For all intents and purposes, there is no such thing as a past or a future—only the present—which is why the legacy of slavery will not go away unless we confront it with a healing process in the present.

Contemporary White Americans are not morally or otherwise responsible for slavery or the failings of their ancestors, any more than the descendants of Africans are responsible for the Africans who supported the European slave trade of their own people. White people are morally responsible for allowing the descendants of slaves to be marginalized, however.

Let all Americans take a few years, a few decades if necessary, and just get out of each other's faces. Let the healing begin with a cooling-off period. Practice mutual respect and common decency, but give the social engineering a rest. Try equality instead of racial integration. Let us choose our neighbors, schools, jobs, and friends on the basis of personal choice, desegregation, equal education, and individual character.

If we repudiate racism and dominance, our ancestors will thank us for allowing their souls to finally rest in peace.

Tony Brown

If we do not adapt as one people . . . we will not survive as a superpower. We have a choice—to grow as a people or to dissolve as a republic.

Tony Brown

It is nice to be regarded on a par with a great white man—now that's funny!

Richard Pryor (responding to the announcement
that he would receive the Kennedy Center's first
Mark Twain Prize honoring American humor)

CIVIL RIGHTS

The cost of liberty is less than the price of repression.

W.E.B. DuBois

We of this less-favored race realize that our future lies chiefly in our hands. . . . And we are struggling on, attempting to show that knowledge can be obtained under difficulties. Neither the old-time slavery, nor continued prejudice need extinguish self-respect, crush manly ambition, or paralyze effort.

Paul Robeson

It is my business not only to tell the guy with the whip hand to go easy on my people, but also to teach my people—all oppressed people—how to prevent that whip hand from being used against them.

Paul Robeson

Friends, we are glad to have made you happy. We hope you have enjoyed us. This is the last time I shall play Louisville [Kentucky], because the management refuses to let people like us sit by people like you. Maybe after the war, we shall have democracy and I can return.

Katherine Dunham (after a
dance performance in 1944)

I think *Brown v. Board of Education* demonstrates that law can also change social patterns. Provided it is adequately enforced, law can change things for the better; moreover, it can change the hearts of men; law has an educational function also.

Thurgood Marshall

I won't "have it made" until the most underprivileged Negro in Mississippi can live in equal dignity with anyone else in America.

Jackie Robinson

Why, of all the multitudinous groups in this country, [do] you have to single out the Negroes and give them this separate treatment? It can't be because of slavery in the past, because there are very few groups in this country that haven't had slavery some place back in the history of their group. It can't be color, because there are Negroes as white as drifted snow, with blue eyes, and they are just as segregated as the colored man. The only thing it can be is an inherent determination that the people who were formerly in slavery, regardless of anything else, shall be kept as near that state as possible.

Thurgood Marshall

When people ask why a separate black law organization is needed at this late date, the answer is simple. It's not that late.

Thurgood Marshall

There is no easy walk to freedom anywhere, and many of us will have to pass through the valley of the shadow of death again and again before we reach the mountaintop of our desires.

Nelson Mandela

It is not a case of our people . . . wanting either separation or integration. The use of these words actually clouds the real picture. The 22 million Afro-Americans don't seek either separation or integration. They seek recognition and respect as human beings.

Malcolm X

Free speech is intended to protect the controversial and even outrageous word; and not just comforting platitudes too mundane to need protection.

Colin Powell

The right of every American to first-class citizenship is the most important issue of our time.

Jackie Robinson

The American ideal, after all, is that everyone should be as much alike as possible.

James Baldwin

I swear to the Lord
I still can't see
Why democracy means
Everybody but me.

Langston Hughes

Civil rights is not by any means the only issue that concerns me—nor, I think any other Negro. As Americans, we have as much at stake in this country as anyone else. But since effective participation in a democracy is based upon enjoyment of basic freedoms that everyone else takes for granted, we need make no apologies for being especially interested in catching up on civil rights.

Jackie Robinson

One of the hardest things in life is having words in your heart that you can't utter.

James Earl Jones

I don't think that I or any other Negro, as an American citizen, should have to ask for anything that is rightfully his. We are demanding that we just be given the things that are rightfully ours and that we're not looking for anything else.

Jackie Robinson

Of my two "handicaps," being female put many more obstacles in my path than being black.

Shirley Chisholm

Negroes aren't seeking anything which is not good for the nation as well as ourselves. In order for America to be 100 percent strong—economically, defensively, and morally—we cannot afford the waste of having second-and-third-class citizens.

Jackie Robinson

Leadership should be born out of the understanding of the needs of those who would be affected by it.

Marian Anderson

People are more easily led than driven.

David Harold Fink

Leadership has a harder job to do than just choose sides. It must bring sides together.

Jesse Jackson

If the First Amendment means anything, it means that the state has no business telling a man, sitting alone in his own house, what books he may read or what films he may watch.

Thurgood Marshall

Mere access to the courthouse doors does not by itself assure a proper functioning of the adversary process.

Thurgood Marshall

This is a great day for the Negro. This is democracy's finest hour.

Adam Clayton Powell, Jr. (on the Brown v. Board of Education *decision, 1954)*

Two months ago I had a nice apartment in Chicago. I had a good job. I had a son. When something happened to the Negroes in the South, I said, "That's their business, not mine." Now I know how wrong I was. The murder of my son has shown me that what happens to any of us, anywhere in the world, had better be the business of us all.

Mamie Bradley

We want to be in control of our lives. Whether we are jungle fighters, craftsmen, company men, gamesmen, we want to be in control. And when the government erodes that control, we are not comfortable.

Barbara Jordan

Concerning non-violence, it is criminal to teach a man not to defend himself when he is the constant victim of brutal attacks.

Malcolm X

The common goal of 22 million Afro-Americans is respect as human beings, the God-given right to be a human being. Our common goal is to obtain the human rights that America has been denying us. We can never get civil rights in America until our human rights are first restored. We will never be recognized as citizens there until we are first recognized as humans.

Malcolm X

The majority of the American people still believe that every single individual in this country is entitled to just as much respect, just as much dignity, as every other individual.

Barbara Jordan

You can't separate peace from freedom because no one can be at peace unless he has his freedom.

Malcolm X

Affirmative action is a betrayal of the principles of the civil rights movement.

Alan Keyes

The Negro revolution is controlled by foxy white liberals, by the government itself. But the Black Revolution is controlled only by God.

Malcolm X

We've made a lot of progress—it's dangerous not to say so. Because if we say so, we tell young people, implicitly or explicitly, that there can be no change. Then they compute: "You mean the life and death and work of Malcolm X and Martin King, the Kennedys, Medgar Evers, Fannie Lou Hamer, the life and struggle of Rosa Parks—they did all that and nothing has changed? Well then, what the hell am I doing? There's no point for me to do anything." The truth is, a lot has changed—for the good. And it's gonna keep getting better, according to how we put our courage forward, and thrust our hearts forth.

Maya Angelou

I believe in the brotherhood of man, all men, but I don't believe in brotherhood with anybody who doesn't want brotherhood with me. I believe in treating people right, but I'm not going to waste my time trying to treat somebody right who doesn't know how to return the treatment.

Malcolm X

If violence is wrong in America, violence is wrong abroad. If it is wrong to be violent defending black women and black children and black babies and black men, then it is wrong for America to draft us, and make us violent abroad in defense of her. And if it is right for America to draft us, and teach us how to be violent in defense of her, then it is right for you and me to do whatever is necessary to defend our own people right here in this country.

Malcolm X

I know we have made some progress over the years, but I know we also have to continue. We can't be too satisfied, because we'll become complacent. . . . There is still racism among other people who haven't quite made up their minds that we're all human beings and we should be treated equally.

Rosa Parks

I want to be a man on the same basis and level as any white citizen. I want to exercise, and in full, the same rights as the white American. I want to be eligible for employment exclusively on the basis of my skills and employability, and for housing solely on my capacity to pay.

Ralph Bunche

I have the audacity to believe that people everywhere can have three meals a day for their bodies, education and culture for their minds, and dignity, equality, and freedom for their spirits. I believe that what self-centered men have torn down, men other-centered can build up. I still believe that one day mankind will bow before the altars of God and be crowned triumphant over war and bloodshed, and non-violent redemptive good will proclaim the rule of the land.

Martin Luther King, Jr.

An unjust law is a code that a numerical or power majority group compels a minority group to obey but does not make binding on itself. . . . One who breaks an unjust law must do so openly, lovingly, and with a willingness to accept the penalty.

Martin Luther King, Jr.

A man has to act like a brother before you can call him a brother.

Malcolm X

Freedom is not free.

Martin Luther King, Jr.

The price of freedom is death.

Malcolm X

Freedom always entails danger.

W.E.B. DuBois

When we let freedom ring, when we let it ring from every village and every hamlet, from every state and every city, we will be able to speed up that day when all of God's children, black men and white men, Jews and Gentiles, Protestants and Catholics, will be able to join hands and sing in the words of the old Negro spiritual, "Free at last! Free at last! Thank God almighty, we are free at last!"

Martin Luther King, Jr.

When you respect the intelligence of black people in this country as being equal to that of whites, then you'll realize that the reaction of the black man to oppression will be the same as the reaction of the white man to oppression.

Malcolm X

Once our freedom struggle is lifted from the confining civil-rights label to the level of human rights, our struggle then becomes internationalized.

Malcolm X

There are Negroes who will never fight for freedom. . . . There are Negroes who will seek profit for themselves before the struggle. . . . No one can pretend that because a people may be oppressed, every individual member is virtuous and worthy.

Martin Luther King, Jr.

I believe in the brotherhood of all men, but I don't believe in wasting brotherhood on anyone who doesn't want to practice it with me. Brotherhood is a two-way street.

Malcolm X

If you knew him you would know why we must honor him: Malcolm was our manhood, our living black manhood. This was his meaning to his people. And in honoring him, we honor the best in ourselves. . . . However much we may have differed with him or with each other about him and his value as a man, let his going from us serve only to bring us together now. . . . Consigning these mortal remains to earth, the common mother of all, secure in the knowledge that what we place in the ground is no more now a man—but a seed—which, after the winter of our discontent, will come forth again to meet us. And we will know him then for what he was and is—a prince—our own black shining prince who didn't hesitate to die, because he loved us so.

Ossie Davis (in his eulogy for Malcolm X, 1965)

Today it is the Negro artist who does *not* speak out who is considered to be out of line.

Paul Robeson

We been saying freedom for six years and we ain't got nothin'. What we gonna start saying now is "Black Power!"

Stokely Carmichael

The civil-rights direction of protest is dead. Now we must concentrate on control—economic and political power.

Marion Barry

I grew up in a small, segregated southern town, but the oppression there was nothing compared to the oppression I saw in the big-city black ghetto.

Wilma Rudolph

Like anybody, I would like to live a long life. Longevity has its place. But I'm not concerned about that just now. I just want to do God's will. And He's allowed me to go up to the mountain. And I've looked over. And I have seen the promised land.

Martin Luther King, Jr.

All token blacks have the same experience. I have been pointed at as a solution to things that have not *begun* to be solved, because pointing at us token blacks eases the conscience of millions, and I think this is dreadfully wrong.

Leontyne Price

On the road to equality, there is no better place for blacks to detour around American values than in its forgoing its example in the treatment of its women and the organization of its family life.

Eleanor Holmes Norton

Let me state here and now that the black woman in America can justly be described as slave of a slave.

Francis M. Beal

Racial oppression of black people in America has done what neither class oppression nor sexual oppression with all their perniciousness has ever done: destroyed an entire people and their culture.

Eleanor Holmes Norton

Black people already know they're poor and powerless. They just don't understand the nature of their oppression. They haven't drawn the line from their condition to the *system* of capitalism.

Huey P. Newton

We know the road to freedom has always been stalked by death.

Angela Davis

What black folks are given in the U.S. on the installment plan, as in civil rights bills. Not to be confused with human rights, which are the dignity, stature, humanity, respect, and freedom belonging to all people by right of birth.

Dick Gregory

The oppression of women, like the oppression of blacks, is one of the pillars of the capitalist system of exploitation. The fight to weaken any one of these pillars contributes to weakening the entire structure that victimizes us all.

Willie Mae Reid

Civil Rights is a term that did not evolve out of black culture, but rather, out of American law. As such, it is a term of limitation.

Alice Walker

I feel blacks should stick together economically the way Jewish people do, the way Italian people do, the way Mormons do, and others. It's something we should aim toward.

Reggie Jackson

When people made up their minds that they wanted to be free and took action, then there was a change.

Rosa Parks

When do any of us do enough?

Barbara Jordan

[In the 1960s] people were going to bed Negro and waking up black. There were major psychological changes going on.

Ron Brown

Our black lesbian and bisexual sisters are sisters without cause
or exception and deserve the same honor and respect that we
all deserve. When we place ourselves in a position of judgment,
then we turn ourselves into oppressors.

Julia A. Boyd

It was thrilling to be able to challenge the circumstances in
which black people were confined: to mobilize and raise consciousness, to change the way people saw themselves, blacks
could express themselves. . . . It gives you an unshakable confidence in your ability.

Elaine Brown

E D U C A T I O N

Education is the development of power and ideas. We want our children trained as intelligent human beings should be, and we will fight for all time against any proposal to educate black boys and girls simply as servants and underlings, or simply for the use of other people. They have a right to know, to think, to aspire.

W.E.B. DuBois

There was never a time in my youth, no matter how dark and discouraging the days might be, when one resolve did not continually remain with me, and that was a determination to secure an education at any cost.

Booker T. Washington

We must do something and we must do it now. We must educate the white people out of their two hundred fifty years of slave history.

Ida B. Wells

You go to school, you study about the Germans and the French, but not about your own race. I hope the time will come when you study black history too.

Booker T. Washington

A system of education is not one thing, nor does it have a single definite object, nor is it a mere matter of schools. Education is that whole system of human training within and without the schoolhouse walls, which molds and develops men.

W.E.B. DuBois

[Negro colleges] do not teach Negroes who they are, what they have done, and what they have to do.

Carter G. Woodson

It is very nearly impossible . . . to become an educated person in a country so distrustful of the independent mind.

James Baldwin

In my opinion, Harvard has ruined more Negroes than bad whiskey.

Carter G. Woodson

The quality of strength lined with tenderness is an unbeatable combination, as are intelligence and necessity when unblunted by formal education.

Maya Angelou

I need to learn as much as I can because I know nothing compared to what I need to know.

Muhammad Ali

Education is all a matter of building bridges.

Ralph Ellison

To make me believe that those men who have regulated education in our country have humanity in their hearts, is to make me believe a lie.

Robert Purvis

The learning process is something you can incite, literally incite, like a riot.

Audre Lorde

Without education, you're not going anywhere in this world.

Malcolm X

Students who don't want to pray don't have to and shouldn't, but a moment of silence to focus on something is a good thing.

Those who don't want to focus on the "unnameable" can think about their roller skates or maybe—grateful surprise—they might even think about their homework, and the subject they're studying.

Maya Angelou

You've really got to start hitting the books, because it's no joke out here.

Spike Lee

Education helps one cease being intimidated by strange situations.

Maya Angelou

Schooling is what happens inside the wall of the school, some of which is educational. Education happens everywhere, and it happens from the moment a child is born—some say before—until it dies.

Sara Lawrence Lightfoot

There will always be some curve balls in your life. Teach your children to thrive in that adversity.

Jeanne Moutoussamy-Ashe

Parents have become so convinced educators know what is best for children that they forget that they themselves are really the experts.

Marian Wright Edelman

The function of education is to teach one to think intensively and to think critically. Intelligence plus character—that is the goal of true education.

Martin Luther King, Jr.

You cannot legislate good will—that comes through education.

Malcolm X

Education meant the death of the institution of slavery in this country, and the slave owners took good care that their slaves got none of it.

Nat Love

I just won't buy the idea that a Negro can't get a decent education unless he's in an integrated situation.

Guichard Parris

Most of what we know about Harlem, most of what we have been told about Harlem, has been told by people who have never lived there, or even been through there at less than 75 miles an hour.

Gil Noble

African-American students on predominantly white college campuses are challenged in ways that other students do not experience. Besides being intellectually ready to achieve academic excellence, African-American students at these schools must be self-confident, self-aware, ambitious, and driven by the mind-set of a crusader on a mission.

Erlene B. Wilson

We are in the midst of a renaissance of solid scholarship about African-American social and cultural forms. The bad news is that too many black studies programs have become segregated, ghettoized corners of quasireligious feeling, propagating old racial fantasies and even inventing new ones.

Henry Louis Gates, Jr.

If I wasn't doing this, I'd be teaching fourth grade. I'd be the same person I always wanted to be, the greatest fourth grade teacher, and win the Teacher of the Year award. But I'll settle for twenty-three Emmys and the opportunity to speak to millions of people each day and, hopefully, teach some of them.

Oprah Winfrey

RELIGION

Our creator is the same and never changes despite the names given Him by people here and in all parts of the world.

George Washington Carver

No one can say that Christianity has failed. It has never been tried.

Adam Clayton Powell, Jr.

Brothers and sisters, the white man has brainwashed us black people to fasten our gaze upon a blond-haired, blue-eyed Jesus! We're worshiping a Jesus that doesn't even look like us! Oh yes! Now just bear with me, listen to the teachings of the Messenger of Allah, The Honorable Elijah Muhammad. Now just think of this. The blond-haired, blue-eyed white man has taught you and me to worship a white Jesus, and to shout and sing and pray to this God that's his God, the white man's God. The white man has taught us to shout and sing and pray until we die, to wait until death, for some dreamy heaven-in-the-hereafter, when we're dead, while this white man has his milk and honey in the streets paved with golden dollars here on this earth!

Malcolm X

If we are to go forward, we must go back and rediscover those precious values—that all reality hinges on moral foundations and that all reality has spiritual control.

Martin Luther King, Jr.

Wherever I found religion in my life I found strife, the attempt of one individual or group to rule another in the name of God. The naked will to power seemed always to walk in the wake of a hymn.

Richard Wright

I find it interesting that the meanest life, the poorest existence, is attributed to God's will, but as human beings become more affluent, as their living standard and style begin to ascend the material scale, God descends the scale of responsibility at a commensurate speed.

Maya Angelou

Prayer begins where human capacity ends.

Marian Anderson

There is nothing in our book, the Koran, that teaches us to suffer peacefully. Our religion teaches us to be intelligent. Be peaceful, be courteous, obey the law, respect everyone; but if someone puts his hand on you, send him to the cemetery. That's a good religion.

Malcolm X

God is a means of liberation, and not a means to control others.

James Baldwin

If Christianity had asserted itself in Germany, 6 million Jews would have lived.

Malcolm X

Confronted with the impossibility of remaining faithful to one's beliefs, and the equal impossibility of becoming free of them, one can be driven to the most inhuman excesses.

James Baldwin

As for those who think the Arab world promises freedom, the briefest study of its routine traditional treatment of blacks (slavery) and women (purdah) will provide relief from all illusion. If Malcolm X had been a black woman his last message to the world would have been entirely different. The brotherhood of Moslem men—all colors—may exist there, but part of the glue that holds them together is the thorough suppression of women.

Alice Walker

Anybody can observe the Sabbath, but making it holy surely takes the rest of the week.

Alice Walker

Somewhere in the Bible it say Jesus' hair was like lamb's wool, I say. Well . . . if he came to any of these churches we talking 'bout he'd have to have it conked before anybody paid him any attention. The last thing niggers want to think about they God is that his hair kinky.

Alice Walker

Everybody can be great, because everybody can serve. You don't have to have a college degree to serve. You don't have to make your subject and your verb agree to serve. You don't have to know about Plato and Aristotle to serve. You don't have to know Einstein's Theory of Relativity to serve. You don't have to know the second theory of thermo-dynamics to serve. You only need a heart full of grace. A soul generated by love.

Martin Luther King, Jr.

I feel like a man who has been asleep somewhat and under someone else's control. I feel that what I'm thinking and saying is now for myself. Before it was for and by the guidance of Elijah Muhammad. Now I think with my own mind, sir!

Malcolm X

For 12 long years I lived within the narrow minded confines of the "straightjacket world" created by my strong belief that Elijah Muhammad was a messenger direct from God Himself, and my faith in what I now see to be a pseudo-religious philosophy that he preaches. . . . I shall never rest until I have undone the harm I did to so many well-meaning, innocent Negroes who through my own evangelistic zeal now believe in him even more fanatically and more blindly than I did.

Malcolm X

The reason you can't claim the ultimate power over your own life is because if you could claim it you could give it up. And you can't give it up. A lot of people don't see this, but those famous words, "are endowed by their Creator with certain unalienable rights," what does that word "unalienable" mean? It means that you cannot give them up, that you are not the ultimate authority in determining whether they are yours or not.

And that makes perfect sense, because the rights are not the result of human decision or artifice. They are inherent in your nature as it comes from the hand of God: a determination of His will, not your will. And therefore, in order to keep that claim, and to stand upon it, even in the face of superior force, superior claims of authority in worldly terms, you must rely on the authority of God.

Alan Keyes

Somehow, we have come to the erroneous belief that we are all but flesh, blood, and bones, and that's all. So we direct our values to material things. We become what writer Beah Richards calls "exiled to things": If we have three cars rather than two, we'll live a little longer. If we have four more titles, we'll live longer still. And, especially, if we have more money than the next guy, we'll live longer than he. It's so sad.

There is something more—the spirit, or the soul. I think that

that quality encourages our courtesy and care and our minds. And mercy, and identity.

Maya Angelou

People see God every day, they just don't recognize Him.

Pearl Bailey

I think it pisses God off if you walk by the color purple in a field somewhere and don't notice it.

Alice Walker

Helped are those who create anything at all, for they shall relive the thrill of their own conception and realize a partnership in the creation of the Universe that keeps them responsible and cheerful.

Alice Walker

You're the one that the book [Bible] is talking about who is dead: dead to the knowledge of yourself, dead to the knowledge of your own people, dead to the knowledge of your own God, dead to the knowledge of the devil. Why, you don't even know who the devil is. You think the devil is someone inside the ground that's going to burn you after you're dead. The devil is right here on top of this earth. He's got blue eyes, brown hair, white skin, and he's giving you hell every day. And you're too dead to see it.

Malcolm X

If we can put the names of our faiths aside for the moment and look at principles, we will find a common thread running through all the great religious expressions.

Louis Farrakhan

We do not condemn the preachers as an individual but we condemn what they teach. We urge that the preachers teach the truth, to teach our people the one important guiding rule of conduct—unity of purpose.

Malcolm X

God is man idealized.

LeRoi Jones (Amiri Baraka)

I believe in a religion that believes in freedom. Any time I have to accept a religion that won't let me fight a battle for my people, I say to hell with that religion.

Malcolm X

We live inside this unbelievable cosmos, inside our unbelievable bodies—everything so perfect, everything so in tune. I got to think God had a hand in it.

Ray Charles

I'm sort of a frightened atheist. If the sky were to open up tomorrow, I'd cop out. I'd probably try to con God. There are a few things I'd like to say to Him—but I don't think it can be done by prayer.

Bill Cosby

The greatest responsibility I feel is to my creator and what I try to fulfill for myself is to honor the creation. The fact that I was created a black woman in this lifetime, everything in my life is built around honoring that. I feel a sense of reverence to that. I hold it sacred. And so I am always asking the question, "What do I owe in service having been created a black woman?"

Oprah Winfrey

I am guided by a higher calling. It's not so much a voice as it is a feeling. If it doesn't feel right to me, I don't do it. . . . I am extremely spiritual. I've not gone into this before because it's personal, but faith is the core of my life.

Oprah Winfrey

It isn't until you come to a spiritual understanding of who you are—not necessarily a religious feeling, but deep down, the spirit within—that you can begin to take control. . . . I think there is no life without a spiritual life. And I think that, more and more, people are becoming aware of the spiritual dynamics of life. And for me, it's always about, "Why are you really here? What is your purpose really about? All the stuff that's really going on, what does it really mean?" I think that we've all just kind of gotten lost in believing that things of the exterior, all the things that we acquire, mean more.

Oprah Winfrey

My opposition [to apartheid] is based firmly and squarely on the Bible and on the injunctions of the Christian gospel.

Desmond Tutu

The question isn't where are the blacks in the Bible, but where are the whites?

Cain Hope Felder

Most man-made religion is built on fear. This is my theory. The fear of judgment. The fear of retribution. Our fears come in all shapes and sizes. One of my favorites is the fear of other religions, or other ways of thinking, and this one's at the root of all our problems. I mean, what the fuck were the Crusades all about? I am going to kill you in the name of God. Yeah, yeah, I know God said thou shalt not kill, but this thou is gonna kill thine ass anyway, and thou's gonna do it so you'll know you were killed by thou in God's name. That's the deal. In Ireland and England, Israel and Syria, it cuts the same way: My religion is better, I'm right, so I'm gonna kill you. I'm not even gonna discuss it.

Whoopi Goldberg

T H E   M I L I T A R Y

It is more than unfortunate, it is an injustice, that regiments that have distinguished themselves in the way the 10th Cavalry and the 25th Infantry have done should be reduced from combat service to be menials to white regiments, without chance for training and promotion, and be excluded from other branches of the services. It is merely a pretense that Negroes are accorded the same treatment in the United States Army as is given white troops. It never has been the case and is not now so.

Major Robert Russa Moton
(letter to Herbert Hoover, 1931)

We want all black men to be exempt from military service.
Black Panther Party platform

Somebody kept trying to tell me everything was going to be all right because I'd most likely be brought in [to World War II] as a musician and wouldn't have to do any fighting. But I told them I wasn't going anywhere. I said I ain't going to take all that training and stuff. I ain't going out on them maneuvers jumping in foxholes with them goddamn snakes and things out there in them swamps. I said I wouldn't and I meant that.

Count Basie

In 1941, the Army still regarded all blacks as totally inferior to whites—somewhat less than human, and certainly incapable of contributing positively to its combat mission.

Benjamin O. Davis, Jr.

During World War II, blacks were not permitted to serve in the U.S. Air Service, an elite officer flying corps. It was thought that black officers giving orders to white enlisted men would create social problems. Despite these opinions, [Tuskegee Institute President] Dr. Patterson invited Alfred "Chief" Anderson to Tuskegee Institute in 1940 to start a flight training program. "Chief" was the first black to receive a commercial pilot license in 1929 and [was] the father of black aviation. First Lady Eleanor Roosevelt, in a public show of support and confidence, came to Tuskegee to be flown by flight trainer "Chief" Anderson. Despite her recommendations to the President, the strong opposition and public debate regarding the "fitness" of blacks to serve continued. However, in late spring of '41, B.O. Davis, Jr., received orders to Tuskegee. Subsequently, on July 10, 1941, the War Department announced that "the first class of ten colored aviation cadets would begin training at Tuskegee Air

Force Base." Once trained, the cadets would serve with the newly activated all-black 99th Pursuit Squadron. Tuskegee was delighted and Dr. Patterson, the school's third president, secured money from the Rosenwald fund to purchase land for what would later be known as Moton Field. A school dormitory housed the trainees. "For the next seven months, I immersed myself in the miracle of flight. In December we got the news . . . it was a Sunday afternoon . . . I was at Tuskegee Institute having a quiet dinner in a restaurant . . . when it was learned . . . the Japanese had bombed Pearl Harbor."

Benjamin O. Davis, Jr.

However, it was not until April 15, 1943, that they were deployed. Under the command of General B.O. Davis, Jr., the 99th Pursuit Squadron and the 332d Fighter Group served with distinction. Over the course of the war . . . 450 black fighter pilots fought in the aerial war over North Africa, Sicily, and Europe, flying P-40, P-39, P-47, and P-51-type aircraft. Four squadrons . . . were designated the 332nd Fighter Group. These valiant men flew 15,553 sorties and completed 1,578 bomber-escort missions over Europe with the 12th Tactical U.S. Army Air Force. They destroyed 409 enemy aircraft . . . theirs was the only squadron to sink a destroyer with gunfire. These brave men were called the *"Schwartze Vogelmenschen"* (Black Birdmen) by the Germans . . . who both respected and feared them. White bomber crews are reported to have reverently referred to them as the Black Red Tail Angels because of their reputation for not losing a single bomber to enemy fighters in 200 escort bombing missions. . . . This record, historians believe, is unmatched by any other unit.

The Pride Edition, March 1990
Tuskegee News

POLITICS

You don't have a peaceful revolution. You don't have a turn-the-other-cheek revolution. There's no such thing as a nonviolent revolution. Revolution is bloody. Revolution is hostile. Revolution knows no compromise. Revolution overturns and destroys everything that gets in its way.

Malcolm X

Naturally, any decision to join a revolutionary movement involves a certain kind of commitment. And naturally, this kind of commitment cannot be made blindly. I am grateful that I had [my husband] Lennie [who happened to be white] to help me make this decision. When Jim Baldwin called me in California and asked me to come to that now "famous" (or "infamous") meeting with Robert Kennedy, the Attorney General, I was torn, for many reasons. First of all, I hate flying. Secondly, although

I have my own opinions about the question, I was not sure what I could contribute to a meeting of that sort (although I had always felt that the Attorney General was someone whom we could approach). Last, and most important, I knew that my commitment could not stop there. When Lennie and I discussed my going, he settled the question by saying, "Go ahead. If you don't go, maybe you won't love *me* anymore."

Lena Horne

Who are the nonvoters? By and large, they are poor and low-income people, including Negroes. They are the people who get the worst deal in this society. On the other hand, those who vote generally have higher incomes and better educations. They get the best deal—which is why they vote. They have their stake and they mean to keep it.

Bayard Rustin

Nonvoting is a fruitless temper tantrum.

Bruce Wright

Any honest examination of the national life proves how far we are from the standard of human freedom with which we began. The recovery of this standard demands of everyone who loves this country a hard look at himself, for the greatest achievements must begin somewhere, and they always begin with the person. If we are not capable of this examination, we may yet become one of the most distinguished and monumental failures in the history of nations.

James Baldwin

All partisan movements add to the fullness of our understanding of society as a whole. They never detract; or, in any case, one must not allow them to do so. Experience adds to experience.

Alice Walker

We know we have to have political clout if we want economic empowerment. And we have that clout if we mobilize the black vote. There are 17 million blacks of voting age, but only 10 million are registered, and only 7 million vote.

John E. Jacob

At present, our country needs women's idealism and determination, perhaps more in politics than anywhere else.

Shirley Chisholm

I guess you'd call me an independent, since I've never identified myself with one party or another in politics. . . . I always decide my vote by taking as careful a look as I can at the actual candidates and issues themselves, no matter what the party label.

Jackie Robinson

If you're going to play the game [politics] properly, you'd better know every rule.

Barbara Jordan

Liberalism seems to be related to the distance people are from the problem.

Whitney M. Young, Jr.

There is little place in the political scheme of things for an independent, creative personality, for a fighter. Anyone who takes that role must pay a price.

Shirley Chisholm

Whenever the media talks about [Jesse Jackson], it becomes a black and white issue as opposed to the contributions he can make to this country.

Stevie Wonder

This country can ill afford to continue to function using less than half of its human resources, brain power, and kinetic energy.

Barbara Jordan

[The U.S. Welfare system is] a concept that emphasizes human needs while neglecting human capacities. It stresses individual helplessness and weakness, undermining the sense of personal responsibility. It justifies ever greater concentrations of power in the hands of the state, leaving people each day more powerless to effect and improve their own condition. This bad concept leads to institutions and policies that disable individual initiative, motivation, and creativity. Faced with political and social structures that embody the assumption of individual impotence, individuals acquire the passive habits and expectations that go with it.

Alan Keyes

[Democrats] don't have the same intellectual firmament, they're not alive and well like the Republican Party is.

Colin Powell

Do they ever ask us before they raise taxes? . . . I say let's not wait to see if their budget can take it. Let's just cut the taxes and have them figure it out like we have to figure it out after they take our money.

Alan Keyes

My faith in the Constitution is whole, it is complete, it is total, and I am not going to sit here and be an idle spectator to the diminuation, the subversion, the destruction of the Constitution.

Barbara Jordan

Forgive me, but I'm not an expert on these matters [such as welfare reform] yet, but it seems like the Congress is not expert on these matters yet, either.

Colin Powell

How do we create a harmonious society out of so many kinds of people? The key is tolerance—the one value that is indispensable in creating community.

Barbara Jordan

If the society today allows wrongs to go unchallenged, the impression is created that those wrongs have the approval of the majority.

Barbara Jordan

Politicians start wars. Soldiers fight and die in them.

Colin Powell

[Jesse Jackson] is a great orator. But I don't know if he has the political skills from his background that it takes to be president [of the United States].

Arsenio Hall

So now Jesse Jackson doesn't run for president anymore—or, if he threatens to, nobody seems to care. He wasn't working for a television station, so there was no one to fire him, but we stopped taking him seriously. Jesse Jackson's punishment was that the people who believed in him no longer do. He's got some talk show, somewhere, and he turns up on the news and makes his speeches, and we listen with a quarter of an ear.

Whoopi Goldberg

Black mayors are expected to control black crime, particularly that affecting whites.

Derrick Bell

I think that this [1992 Supreme Court confirmation] hearing today is a travesty. . . . And from my standpoint as a black American, it is a high-tech lynching for uppity blacks who in any way deign to think for themselves.

Clarence Thomas

What a bitter twist of fate. [Clarence Thomas], who had, in hustling the favors of [George] Bush and the right-wingers who currently controlled America—and who had disparaged and ridiculed Thurgood Marshall, Walter White, James Weldon Johnson, Roy Wilkins, and others who wiped out lynching—was now crying "lynching" to justify his confirmation. This child of Georgia poverty who had exhorted blacks never to fall back on cries of "racism" was shouting "racist lynching" in the most galling of ways.

Carl T. Rowan

Clarence Thomas is wrong on every possible question we can think of that is important to our future survival as a people.

Pearl Cleage

I've purposefully stayed away from politics. I'm only interested in presenting issues, so that I can allow people to see the truth for themselves. I've never been very good at interviewing political figures because I've never been able to penetrate their agenda to get to what I thought was the truth.

Oprah Winfrey

[New York City] Mayor [Rudy] Giuliani says blacks have a fear of his administration. On that, he's right. He says he does not know the reason blacks feel the way they do. On that, he's got to be kidding.

Earl Caldwell

While I believe that independent politics is where the black community and others need to go, the Democratic Party is where they are.

Lenore Fulani

I don't care how many people our presidents have slept with. I truly don't. It doesn't take away from who they are or what they're about or what they might accomplish. Just because a guy gets his tip wet once in a while, it doesn't make him a bad president. It doesn't even make him a bad guy. It's just part of the human package. . . .

Hey, Clinton copped to smoking that joint (although I could have done without the questionable inhaling crap, but maybe he'll cop to that one day too). He copped to Gennifer Flowers, and the Republicans may even find something for him to cop to in Whitewater or his campaign-financing mess. And we'll make him cop to every last piece of indecision or cowardice or bad judgment, and in the end what will count is whether or not we think this man has the stones and the heart and the mind to lead this country in a positive direction. Do we believe what he stands for, and in what he's trying to accomplish? Or do we just want to slap another scarlet letter on yet another person just to help us feel a little better about ourselves?

Decide, people. Decide.

Whoopi Goldberg

I view Bill Clinton as the first black president. He spends a hundred-dollar bill, they hold it up to the light.

Chris Rock

A B O R T I O N

If men could get pregnant, abortion would be a sacrament.

Florence Kennedy

I am appalled at the ethical bankruptcy of those who preach a "right to life" that means, under present social policies, a bare existence in utter misery for many poor women and their children.

Thurgood Marshall

Whether you are choosing to have a baby out of wedlock or choosing to get an abortion, what is really wrong in that situation is that there is something deeply wrong with your moral compass and you need some help.

Alan Keyes

The implication of *Roe v. Wade* is that we human beings decide not only on the value, but even on the humanity, of that life in the womb, of human life. In doing so, what is it that we do, according to our own American creed? It's clear; in that creed it is clearly stated: We hold these truths to be self-evident; that all men are created equal; that they are endowed—not by mother's decision, father's decision, Congress's decision, court's decision, or any human decision, but by God—with their un-alienable rights: the bedrock premise of American life. Which makes a lot of people uncomfortable. And when I say what I'm about to say, they all try to come up in arms against me, and accuse me of imposing religion or something on American life. No I don't. I'm just looking at the principle, right there in front of us. That principle on which everything rests, for which there has been and is no substitute as the foundation of our free way of life. And that principle clearly respects, clearly relies upon, the sovereignty of God.

Alan Keyes

If we can't preserve the privacy of our right to procreate, I can't imagine what rights we will be able to protect.

Faye Wattleton

[Right-to-lifers] love little babies as long as they are in somebody else's uterus.

Dr. Joycelyn Elders

SPORTS

I made a lot of mistakes out of the ring, but I never made any in it.

Jack Johnson

I made the most of my ability and I did my best with my title.

Joe Louis

Champions aren't made in gyms. Champions are made from something they have deep inside them—a desire, a dream, a vision. They have to have last-minute stamina, they have to be a little faster, they have to have the skill and the will. But the will must be stronger than the skill.

Muhammad Ali

The game is my wife. It demands loyalty and responsibility, and it gives me back fulfillment and peace.

Michael Jordan

Ask any athlete: We all hurt at times. I'm asking my body to go through seven different tasks. To ask it not to ache would be too much.

Jackie Joyner-Kersee

It's just a job. Grass grows, birds fly, waves pound the sand. I beat people up.

Muhammad Ali

The fight is won or lost far away from witnesses. It is won behind the scenes, in the gym, and out there on the road, long before I dance under those lights.

Muhammad Ali

Baseball was just a part of my life. Thank God that I didn't allow a sport or a business or any part of my life to dominate me completely. . . . I felt that I had my time in athletics and that was it.

Jackie Robinson

Most of us who aspire to be tops in our fields don't really consider the amount of work required to stay tops.

Althea Gibson

I never wanted them to forget Babe Ruth. I just wanted them to remember Henry Aaron.

Hank Aaron

My heroes are and were my parents. I can't see having anyone else as my heroes.

Michael Jordan

Fans don't boo nobodies.

Reggie Jackson

I have always felt that although someone may defeat me, and I strike out in a ball game, the pitcher on the particular day was the best player. But I know when I see him again, I'm going to be ready for his curve ball. Failure is a part of success. There is no such thing as a bed of roses all your life. But failure will never stand in the way of success if you learn from it.

Hank Aaron

For a time, at least, I was the most famous person in the entire world.

Jesse Owens

Even when I was little, I was big.

William "Refrigerator" Perry

I don't believe that I personally have been changed by the money. The bad thing is people assume you've changed because now you have money.

Shaquille O'Neal

[During the big July 4, 1910 fight] I looked about me and scanned that sea of white faces. I felt the auspiciousness of the occasion. There were few men of my own race among the spectators. I realized that my victory in this event meant more than on any previous occasion. It wasn't just the championship that was at stake—it was my own honor—and to a degree, the honor of my race. I was well aware of all these things and I sensed that most of that great audience was hostile to me, but I was cool and perfectly at ease. I never had any doubt of the outcome.

Jack Johnson

Until the time comes when a Negro player can go out and argue his point as well as any other ball player, I hope that all of us are able to bite our tongues and just play ball.

Jackie Robinson

I didn't want to hurt him more than I had to.

Joe Louis

When I played against white players in the early days, the linesmen didn't always call them out. I learned that there was no use complaining, but I also learned that I could win anyway.

Arthur Ashe

The [boxing] ring was the only place a Negro could whip a white man and not be lynched.

Malcolm X

Racism is not an excuse to not do the best you can.

Arthur Ashe

Where do you think I would be next week if I didn't know how to shout and holler and make the public sit up and take notice? I would be poor, for one thing, and I would probably be down in Louisville, Kentucky (my home town), washing windows or running an elevator an' saying "yes suh" and "no suh" and knowing my place. Instead of that, I'm saying I'm one of the highest paid athletes in the world, and that I'm the greatest fighter in the world.

Muhammad Ali

Everywhere I go, I'm being honored and I don't really deserve it. It makes me scared.

Muhammad Ali

I'm the world champion but I don't feel any different than that fan over there. I'll still walk in the ghettoes, answer questions, kiss babies. I didn't marry a blonde or go nude in the movies. I'll never forget my people.

Muhammad Ali

Too many victories weaken you. The defeated can rise up stronger than the victor.

Muhammad Ali

I don't doubt what my ability to play baseball has done for me.

Hank Aaron

I hated the sight on TV of big, clumsy, lumbering heavyweights plodding, stalking each other like two Frankenstein monsters, clinging, slugging toe to toe. I knew I could do it better. I would be as fast as a lightweight, circle, dance, shuffle, hit, and move. Dance again, and make an art out of it.

Muhammad Ali

Sports and politics do mix. Behind the scenes, the two are as inextricably interwoven as any two issues can be. I'm sure politics are involved when teams get franchises or when cities build stadiums. It is unrealistic to say you shouldn't bring politics into sports.

Arthur Ashe

Being a runner was my biggest goal. Now I'm the fastest woman in the world on a track.

Evelyn Ashford

In sports, especially professional sports, your accomplishments only stand up on their own when you retire.

Darryl Strawberry

I've been called the Jackie Robinson of golf by many newspaper writers over the years, but I'm a little disgusted by the comparison at this point in my life. It's true that I was the first black to break into the all-white PGA tour. Out of nearly 400 professional golfers in this country, there are only seven blacks? That's so far out of line that it's ridiculous.

Charles Sifford

I like the image Michael [Jordan] has made for himself, an image of a good guy who gets involved in the community, likes kids, has a lot of self-confidence, but isn't just some crazy egomaniac.

Shaquille O'Neal

Once I get the ball, you're at my mercy. There's nothing you can say or do about it. I own the ball, I own the game, I own the guy guarding me.

Michael Jordan

For all his marvelous gifts, [Michael] Jordan wasn't inclined to use his visibility to carry a torch for equal rights and ending racism.

William C. Rhoden

There's no doubt that fans are part of the life of an athlete. I could spend 24 hours a day reading the mail and responding to it, but then I wouldn't have any time left to play basketball.

Shaquille O'Neal

S K I L L S

Excellence is the name of the game, no matter what color or what country you're from. If you are the best at what you're doing, then you have my admiration and respect.

Judith Jamison

Black minds and talent have skills to control a spacecraft or scalpel with the same finesse and dexterity with which they control a basketball.

Ronald McNair

I was raised to believe that excellence is the best deterrent to racism or sexism. And that's how I operate my life.

Oprah Winfrey

Tremendous amounts of talent are being lost to our society just because that talent wears a skirt.

Shirley Chisholm

The hardest work in the world is being out of work.

Whitney M. Young, Jr.

I want to do everything. I want to be the first black President. Give me about ten years, I'm going to run for President. If I can squeeze in an N.B.A. championship before that, I'll do it.

Will Smith

I'm a natural interviewer. I don't do a lot of preparation. I don't like to work from a script. It confuses me. I'm best when I can sit down, have a conversation, and develop some sort of insight. . . . Every day is a challenge. It's simply important to me to be the best I can be. And in this business, if you're good, it speaks for itself.

Oprah Winfrey

The reason I became ballerina of the Metropolitan Opera was because I couldn't be topped. You don't get there *because*, you get there *in spite of*.

Janet Collins

Practically, affirmative action is probably necessary. But I would not want to know that I received a job simply because I am black. Affirmative action tends to undermine the spirit of individual initiative.

Arthur Ashe

THE ARTS

The Negro artist works against an undertow of sharp criticism and misunderstanding from his own group and unintentional bribes from the whites. . . . "O, be respectable, write about nice people, show how good we are," say the Negroes. . . . "Be stereotyped, don't go too far, don't shatter our illusions about you, don't amuse us too seriously. We will pay you," say the whites.

Langston Hughes

The written word is the only record we will have of this our present, or our past, to leave behind for future generations. It would be a shame if that written word in its creative form were to consist largely of defeat and death.

Langston Hughes

The road for the serious black artist, then, who would produce a racial art is most certainly rocky and the mountain is high.

Langston Hughes

A dark man shall see dark days. Bop comes out of them dark days. Folks who ain't suffered much cannot play bop, neither appreciate it.

Langston Hughes

An artist must be free to choose what he does, certainly, but he must also never be afraid to do what he might choose.

Langston Hughes

One of the most promising of young Negro poets said to me once, "I want to be a poet—not a Negro poet," meaning, I believe, "I want to write like a white poet," meaning subconsciously, "I would like to be a white poet," meaning behind that, "I would like to be white." And I was sorry the young man said that, for no great poet has ever been afraid of being himself.

Langston Hughes

The new racial poetry of the Negro is the expression of something more than experimentation in a new technique. It marks the birth of a new racial consciousness and self-conception. It lacks apology, the wearying appeals to pity, and the conscious philosophy of defense. In being itself it reveals its greatest charm; and in accepting its distinctive life, invests it with a new meaning.

Charles S. Johnson

I developed an isolation from the audience that was actually only a sophisticated cover for hostility. But the audience didn't see it; they were too busy seeing their own preconceived images of a Negro woman. The image that I myself chose to give them was of a woman whom they could not reach. I think this is why I rarely speak to an audience. I am too proud to let *them* think they can have any personal contact with me. They get the singer, but they are not going to get the woman. I think many Negro performers feel much the same way and they find their own methods of letting people know it. In other words, we all find our own means of rebellion.

Lena Horne

Any writer, I suppose, feels that the world into which he was born is nothing less than a conspiracy against the cultivation of his talent.

James Baldwin

I'm a musician at heart, I know I'm not really a singer. I couldn't compete with real singers. But I sing because the public buys it.

Nat "King" Cole

The primary distinction of the artist is that he must actively cultivate that state which most men, necessarily, must avoid: the state of being alone.

James Baldwin

Writing saved me from the sin and inconvenience of violence.

Alice Walker

It is only in his music, which Americans are able to admire because a protective sentimentality limits their understanding of it, that the Negro in America has been able to tell his story.

James Baldwin

Maybe fifty years after I'm dead, my music will be appreciated.

Scott Joplin

It is healthier, in any case, to write for the adults one's children will become than for the children one's "mature" critics often are.

Alice Walker

I look for that seamlessness between art and reality. When I can find those scenes, that's when I'm most interested. And when the dialogue sounds like people speak, and when what the dialogue conveys is crystal clear to me, then they've got me— they've really got me.

Sidney Poitier

The responsibility of a writer is to excavate the experience of the people who produced him.

James Baldwin

I have never been able to analyze the qualities that the audience contributes to a performance. The most important, I think, are sympathy, open-mindedness, expectancy, faith, and a certain support to your effort. I know that my career could not have been what it is without all these things, which have come from many people. The knowledge of the feelings other people have expended on me has kept me going when times were hard. That knowledge has been a responsibility, a challenge, and an inspiration. It has been the path to development and growth. The faith and confidence of others in me have been like shining, guiding stars.

Marian Anderson

Art is the only thing you cannot punch a button for. You must do it the old-fashioned way. Stay up and really burn the midnight oil. There are no compromises.

Leontyne Price

The last thing I want to be is a rich black superstar. I just want to act.

James Earl Jones

Writing has made me a better man. It has put me in contact with those fleeting moments which prove the existence.

Ishmael Reed

I have learned as much about writing about my people by listening to blues and jazz and spirituals as I have by reading novels.

Ernest J. Gaines

You've got to find some way of saying it without saying it.

Duke Ellington

I try to do what has never been done before.

Ishmael Reed

I acknowledge immense debt to the griots [tribal poets] of Africa—where today it is rightly said that when a griot dies, it is as if a library has burned to the ground.

Alex Haley

When I read great literature, great drama, speeches, or sermons, I feel that the human mind has not achieved anything greater than the ability to share feelings and thoughts through language.

James Earl Jones

No one says a novel has to be one thing. It can be anything it wants to be, a vaudeville show, the six o'clock news, the mumblings of wild men saddled by demons.

Ishmael Reed

Regardless of the criticisms I receive from the left, the right and the middle, I think it's important to maintain a prolific writing jab, as long as my literary legs hold up.

Ishmael Reed

I look at my books the way parents look at their children. The fact that one becomes more successful than the others doesn't make me love the less successful one any less.

Alex Haley

The conservative right has decided that artists are apart from the people. That's ridiculous! I mean, at our best the writer, painter, architect, actor, dancer, folksinger—we are the people. We come out of the people, and remain in the people. . . . What we ought to be doing is singing in the parks, talking to children, going to gatherings of parents, doing whatever it is we do—dancing, reading poetry, performing—all the time, so that people know, "These artists are my people—you can't kill them, you can't stop them." We then re-establish our footing with the people. All artists must do that, or we will be defanged.

Maya Angelou

There is hardly any money interest in art, and music will be there when money is gone.

Duke Ellington

The purpose of art is to lay bare the questions which have been hidden by the answers.

James Baldwin

Beyond talent lie all the usual words: discipline, love, luck—but, most of all, endurance.

James Baldwin

Music is the greatest communication in the world. Even if people don't understand the language that you're singing in, they still know good music when they hear it.

Lou Rawls

What success I achieved in the theater is due to the fact that I have always worked just as hard when there were ten people in the house as when there were thousands. Just as hard in Springfield, Illinois, as on Broadway.

Bill "Bojangles" Robinson

I sing about life.

Marvin Gaye

This is the only real concern of the artist, to recreate out of the disorder of life that order which is art.

James Baldwin

I swore to myself that if I ever wrote another book, no one would weep over it; that it would be so hard and deep that they would have to face it without the consolation of tears.

Richard Wright

Commercial rock and roll music is a brutalization of one stream of contemporary Negro church music . . . an obscene looting of a cultural expression.

Ralph Ellison

Certainly Hollywood has been making films lately starring black actors, but the blackness of the character is always the cause of the conflict in the story. Writers and producers seem to think that you need a special reason for a role to be played by a Negro.

Bill Cosby

If you cannot sing a congregational song at full power, you cannot fight in any struggle. It is something you learn. We would sing together, we would invoke the spirit. We would sing about anything we felt. We would sing about why we sing. We would sing, "The reason I sing this song, Lord, I don't want to be lost." We would sing about the abuses we suffered, like not being allowed to vote. We would sing songs of sorrow and of hope.

Dorothy Cotton

Oh, Black known and unknown poets, how often have your auctioned pains sustained us? Who will compute the lonely nights made less lonely by your songs, or by the empty pots made less tragic by your tales?

Maya Angelou

My approach to solving social problems is through the arts; the arts give you a discipline and a structure.

Arthur Mitchell

So Elvis Presley came, strumming a weird guitar and wagging his tail across the continent, ripping off fame and fortune as he scrunched his way, and, like a latter-day Johnny Appleseed, sowing seeds of a new rhythm and style in the white soul of the new white youth of America, whose inner hunger and need was no longer satisfied with the antiseptic white shows and whiter songs of Pat Boone.

Eldridge Cleaver

The most apparent legacies of the African past, even to the contemporary Black American . . . blues, jazz, and the adoption of the Christian religion, all rely heavily on African culture.

LeRoi Jones (Amiri Baraka)

To explore the black experience means that we do not deny the reality and the power of the slave culture; the culture that produced the blues, spirituals, folk songs, work songs, and "jazz." It means that Afro-American life and its myriad styles are expressed and examined in the fullest, most truthful manner possible.

Laurence P. Neal

The most astonishing aspect of the blues is that, though replete with a sense of defeat and downheartedness, they are not intrinsically pessimistic; their burden of woe and melancholy is dialectically redeemed through sheer force of sensuality into an exultant affirmation of life, of love, of sex, of movement, of hope.

Richard Wright

Great art can only be created out of love.

James Baldwin

Blues is joyful. It's a celebration of having overcome bad times.

Joe Williams

There are no wrong notes.

Theolonious Monk

Helped are those who create anything at all, for they shall relive the thrill of their own conception and realize a partnership in the creation of the Universe that keeps them responsible and cheerful.

Alice Walker

A black woman writer who wants to write seriously about contemporary cultural issues and how they are socially constructed is faced with an almost insurmountable communication problem: If she takes a scholarly approach, she will be virtually ignored because black women have no power in that context; if she takes a colloquial "entertainment" approach, then she will be read, but she will be attacked and ostracized.

Michele Wallace

Art is the ability to tell the truth, especially about oneself.

Richard Pryor

Without [Phil] Donahue [my] show wouldn't be possible. He showed that women have an interest in things that affect their lives and not just how to stuff a cabbage. Because of that I have nothing to prove, only to do good shows. . . . I say, he's the king and I just want a little piece of the kingdom.

Oprah Winfrey

Bishop Tutu wouldn't hug Donahue.

Oprah Winfrey

Spike Lee accused Eddie [Murphy]. He said any man who makes a billion dollars should demand more black participation at Paramount. Standing on the outside doing *She's Gotta Have It*, you don't understand the big leagues. If Eddie went in and told [Paramount CEO] Frank Mancuso to do something, he'd tell Eddie to fuck off.

Arsenio Hall

Even someone with Eddie [Murphy's] box office power can't change Hollywood overnight. And that change doesn't occur any quicker if you go to a Caucasian journalist looking to stir up conflict by telling him what you think of your black brother.

It takes time to get things. And you can't demand them: You have to slowly show the need, show them it makes money. 'Cause the bottom line is, there's not as much racism in this town over "You're white and I'm black" as there is over "Show me green." Trust me: The biggest racists in this town will give you anything you want if you show them a profit.

Arsenio Hall (discussing race relations
in Hollywood with Spike Lee)

The bottom line is that I have more blacks behind the camera and in front of the camera than anyone else in the history of talk shows.

Arsenio Hall

Black people don't like unhappy endings. Perhaps we have too many.

Jamaica Kincaid

I don't want to do anything to negatively affect a young kid, regardless of how hard the [rap music] label wants me to be or what the market will bear for me to be . . . if that's gonna cost me some sales, then fine.

Young M.C.

Before I got signed, I read anything I could about the music business—especially about the Motown days when people sold millions of singles and saw no money. . . . I made a point to know what was going on with me contractually.

Toni Braxton

Music is your own experience—your thoughts, your wisdom. If you don't live it, it won't come out of your horn.

Charlie Parker

It is important for African-American writers and directors to develop projects with better characters, so they can have an impact on the images that are being shown.

Steve Sanford

There is not one black person who can "green-light" a television project, who can say, "Yes, let's make that film or put that show on the air."

Tim Reid

Street rap is an unforgivable and unspeakable obscenity that some black entertainers have enriched themselves on by selling music that describes women as "bitches and hos," other blacks as "niggers," and encourages wanton violence against women and the police.

Earl G. Long

E N T E R T A I N M E N T

Being a star made it possible for me to get insulted in places where the average Negro could never hope to go and get insulted.

Sammy Davis, Jr.

The bottom line with me is fun. I don't like stress. People have so much stress in their lives that it's kind of a breath of fresh air to just sit for an hour and a half and watch a movie of somebody who's just having fun. I enjoy life, I enjoy people. And people—black, white, Asian . . . or alien—enjoy that energy.

Will Smith

I was on my way down to Miami . . . I mean They-ami. I was ridin' along in my Cadillac, you know, goin' through one of them little towns in South Carolina. Pass through a red light. One of them big cops come runnin' over to me, say, "Hey, woman, don't you know you went through a red light?" I say, "Yeah, I know I went through a red light." "Well, what did you do that for?" I said, " 'Cause I seen all you white folks goin' on the green light . . . thought the red light was for us!"

"Moms" Mabley

All the jokes in the world are based on a few elemental ideas. The sight of other people in trouble is nearly always funny.

Bert Williams

It's going to be harder for [gay] folks to openly come out and get the work that they want [in Hollywood]. . . . Gay folks will go through stages in the movies like black people did. There was always a tragic mulatto; now there'll be the tragic gay person. At some point we'll just sort of absorb this into our bodies and start dealing with people.

Whoopi Goldberg

Hollywood's a tough town. I look at it like, you're driving on the highway and it's raining, and there's that one car broken down on the side of the road. Hundreds of thousands of cars in perfect working order in every direction, and there's that one car broken down on the side of the road. One day, that's gonna be you. One day, you're going to be that car broken down on the side of the road. And when you are, it's cool, it's okay. Tow truck's gonna come. You're gonna get it fixed, you're gonna be back on the road. You just gotta ride through it.

Will Smith

I was in the music business first, and it's really cutthroat and hard. So I had my ups and downs. Had money, then was broke. I kinda got my footing together before I got into television and the film world. Because this type of attention can make you crazy.

Will Smith

To be absolutely objective, the industry doesn't really have that kind of need for me [any more]. I can play fathers. I can play grandfathers. I can play interesting characters. . . . But that's the nature of being a 72-year-old.

Sidney Poitier

I've got to be a colored funny man, not a funny colored man.

Dick Gregory

"Sorry, we don't serve colored folks here." His reply, "Fine, I don't eat them, just bring me a medium rare hamburger."

Dick Gregory

More than anything else, I would like to be like Nat "King" Cole. He had staying power, something that all people, no matter what color, liked.

Lou Rawls

I don't think I'll do any serious acting; *48 Hours* is about as heavy as I want to get.

Eddie Murphy

I've sung "Ooo Baby Baby" maybe 10 trillion times, but every time I sing that song, I still feel what's happening.

Smokey Robinson

Black audiences respond to their film heroes differently than white audiences respond. Denzel Washington was telling me that he feels a little more cramped. In the cinema, blacks haven't had as many heroes as the white community has had in films; so what happens is everybody who makes it through is carrying the torch for the black community.

Will Smith

There's a pure beauty to Grace Jones. That face of hers is like a chiseled ebony statue.

Billy Dee Williams

Prince has got that raunchy thing, almost like a pimp and a bitch all wrapped up in one image . . . but he's really like his name, a prince of a person when you get to know him.

Miles Davis

I want to be the Martin Luther King of comedy.

Arsenio Hall

Niggers just have a way of telling you stuff and not telling you stuff. Martians would have a difficult time with Niggers. They be translating words, saying a whole lot of things underneath you, all around you . . . that's our comedy.

Richard Pryor

You know, it's all because I wanted to be accepted. That's why I tell jokes. I discovered that people would laugh at my jokes, and that meant they *liked me*, they accepted me. It was even better when they started throwing *money*.

Bill Cosby

[Oprah Winfrey] is an honest, hardworking woman who has developed an unusual amount of caring and courage. [She] is making her journey at what might seem to be a dizzying pace, but it is her pace. She has set her own tempo.

Maya Angelou

Acting is the one thing I always knew I could do.

Whoopi Goldberg

White America has always let us entertain them, but we've never had any real control, any real power. It's a new day, you know, and it's time for us to stop shooting the ball and start owning the court.

Arsenio Hall

The role I played in *Father Hood* was actually written for a man at first and then just a woman. So for me to be able to get it was a milestone. It was the first time I got a role that hadn't been written for a black woman, just a woman.

Halle Berry

It sometimes hurts me that people may think I'm a bitchy diva. . . . That's not who I am.

Mariah Carey

I like Chris Rock. I like that he keeps saying nice things about me. Does he remind me of me? I'm afraid so.

Richard Pryor

My show is not a black show, it's not a show to take over the airwaves. It's a show to say, "Let's share the medium now." . . . Beaver's dead, baby. Beaver's gone. And it's time to let some blacks move into that neighborhood.

Arsenio Hall

Any woman in my life has to deal with the fact that we may finish making love and I may jump up and write down the sounds that we made, and she may hear it on my monologue the next night.

Arsenio Hall

America has become comfortable and literally color-blind in its acceptance and adoration of the blacks who entertain, but it is still stubbornly racist in conceding equitable power to blacks in most other arenas. That shouldn't be surprising. The power to entertain is not quite the same as the power to control.

Audrey Edwards and Craig K. Polite

The last time there was a real funny black TV show was *The Jeffersons*. . . . Cosby was the only funny guy on his show. But every character was funny on *The Jeffersons*. It was just so structurally sound. People don't realize how pioneering a show it was. You had a professional black man *before* Cosby. And for all his faults, George Jefferson never lost his money. And the honesty! Let's face it, there's no such thing as a 50-year-old black man that's not racist and pissed off. You're 50, you rode the back of the bus. *The Jeffersons* was honest about this.

Chris Rock

OPINIONS *and*

PHILOSOPHIES

❖

When I can leave my office in time so that I can spend thirty or forty minutes in spading the ground, in planting seeds, in digging about the plants, I feel that I am coming into contact with something that is giving me strength for the many duties and hard places that await me out in the big world. I pity the man or woman who has never learned to enjoy nature and get strength and inspiration out of it.

Booker T. Washington

A good garden is one of the best family physicians. Have a garden, a little place by the house, even if it's only big enough to throw a dipper over it.

Booker T. Washington

When our thoughts—which bring actions—are filled with hate against anyone, Negro or white, we are in a living hell. That is as real as hell will ever be.

George Washington Carver

Human dignity is more precious than prestige.

Claude McKay

No race can prosper until it learns that there is as much dignity in tilling a field as in writing a poem.

Booker T. Washington

The ignorant are always prejudiced and the prejudiced are always ignorant.

Charles V. Roman

A woman is a woman until the day she dies, but a man's a man only as long as he can.

"Moms" Mabley

If someone hit me on one cheek, I'd tear his head off before he could hit me on the other one.

Paul Robeson

We ourselves have the power to end the terror and win for ourselves peace and security. We have the power of numbers, the power of organization, and the power of spirit.

Paul Robeson

The imperative is to define what is right and do it.

Barbara Jordan

Love, I find, is like singing. Everybody can do enough to satisfy themselves, though it may not impress the neighbors as being very much.

Zora Neale Hurston

Do not call for black power or green power. Call for brain power.

Barbara Jordan

A woman who is willing to be herself and pursue her own potential runs not so much the risk of loneliness as the challenge of exposure to more interesting men—and people in general.

Lorraine Hansberry

I believe in the goodness of a free society. And I believe that society can remain good only as long as we are willing to fight for it—and to fight against whatever imperfections may exist.

Jackie Robinson

The thing that makes you exceptional, if you are at all, is inevitably that which must also make you lonely.

Lorraine Hansberry

Every one has a gift for something, even if it is the gift of being a good friend.

Marian Anderson

Life is not a spectator sport. . . . If you're going to spend your whole life in the grandstand just watching what goes on, in my opinion you're wasting your life.

Jackie Robinson

Rage cannot be hidden, it can only be dissembled. This dissembling deludes the thoughtless, and strengthens rage and adds, to rage, contempt.

James Baldwin

Luck is a matter of preparation meeting opportunity.

Oprah Winfrey

The gift of loneliness is sometimes a radical vision of society or one's people that has not previously been taken into account.

Alice Walker

People who treat other people as less than human must not be surprised when the bread they have cast on the waters comes floating back to them, poisoned.

James Baldwin

Never be the only one, except, possibly, in your own home.

Alice Walker

We have all had the experience of finding that our reactions and perhaps even our deeds have denied beliefs we thought were ours.

James Baldwin

I never intended to become a run-of-the-mill person.

Barbara Jordan

Most of us are about as eager to be changed as we were to be born, and go through our changes in a similar state of shock.

James Baldwin

Self-pity in its early stage is as snug as a feather mattress. Only when it hardens does it become uncomfortable.

Maya Angelou

Voyagers discover that the world can never be larger than the person that is in the world; but it is impossible to foresee this, it is impossible to be warned.

James Baldwin

If you're trying to be the greatest you got to go into it like you *are* the greatest. . . .

Sean "Puffy" Combs

If you apply reason and logic to this career of mine, you're not going to get very far. You simply won't. The journey has been incredible from its beginning. So much of life, it seems to me, is determined by pure randomness.

Sidney Poitier

Words like "freedom," "justice," "democracy" are not common concepts; on the contrary, they are rare. People are not born knowing what these are. It takes enormous and, above all, individual effort to arrive at the respect for other people that these words imply.

James Baldwin

In my music, my plays, my films, I want to carry always this central idea: to be African. Multitudes of men have died for less worthy ideals: it is even more eminently worth living for.

Paul Robeson

It is certain, in any case, that ignorance, allied with power, is the most ferocious enemy justice can have.

James Baldwin

I am invisible, understand, simply because people refuse to see me.

Ralph Ellison

There is always something left to love. And if you haven't learned that, you ain't learned nothing.

Lorraine Hansberry

Hibernation is a covert preparation for a more overt action.

Ralph Ellison

The antidote to hubris, to overweening pride, is irony, that capacity to discover and systematize ideas. Or, as Emerson insisted, the development of consciousness, consciousness, consciousness.

Ralph Ellison

You should always know when you're shifting gears in life. You should leave your era; it should never leave you.

Leontyne Price

[T]here is only one large circle that we march in, around and around, each of us with our own little picture—in front of us—our own little mirage that we think is the future.

Lorraine Hansberry

When morality comes up against profit, it is seldom profit that loses.

Shirley Chisholm

I live a day at a time. Each day I look for a kernel of excitement. In the morning, I say: "What is my exciting thing for today?" Then, I do the day. Don't ask me about tomorrow.

Barbara Jordan

We must exchange the philosophy of excuse—what I am is beyond my control—for the philosophy of responsibility.

Barbara Jordan

Our ability to create has outreached our ability to use wisely the products of our invention.

Whitney M. Young, Jr.

Support the strong, give courage to the timid, remind the indifferent, and warn the opposed.

Whitney M. Young, Jr.

Either you deal with what is the reality, or you can be sure that the reality is going to deal with you.

Alex Haley

Never completely encircle your enemy. Leave him some escape, for he will fight even more desperately if trapped.

Alex Haley

Perpetual optimism is a force multiplier.

Colin Powell

Those that don't got it, can't show it. Those that got it, can't hide it.

Zora Neale Hurston

Nothing that God ever made is the same thing to more than one person. That is natural. There is no single face in nature, because every eye that looks upon it, sees it from its own angle. So every man's spice-box seasons his own food.

Zora Neale Hurston

I want a busy life, a just mind, and a timely death.

Zora Neale Hurston

A spirit of harmony can only survive if each of us remembers, when bitterness and self-interest seem to prevail, that we share a common destiny.

Barbara Jordan

Justice of right is always to take precedence over might.

Barbara Jordan

It is a time for martyrs now, and if I am to be one, it will be for the cause of brotherhood. That's the only thing that can save this country.

Malcolm X

It is reason and not passion which must guide our deliberations, guide our debate, and guide our decision.

Barbara Jordan

What the people want is very simple. They want an America as good as its promise.

Barbara Jordan

Wanting something is not enough. You must hunger for it. Your motivation must be absolutely compelling in order to overcome the obstacles that will invariably come your way.

Les Brown

Nothing is easy to the unwilling.

Nikki Giovanni

You've got to make haste while it's still light of day. My godmother used to say, "I don't want to rust out, I just want to work out." If you stand still long enough, people will throw dirt on you.

Ben Vereen

Where there is no vision, the people perish.

James Baldwin

Think like a queen. A queen is not afraid to fail. Failure is another stepping-stone to greatness.

Oprah Winfrey

Respect commands itself and it can neither be given nor withheld when it is due.

Eldridge Cleaver

The best preparation for tomorrow is to do your best today.

Lou Gossett, Jr.

My great hope is to laugh as much as I cry; to get my work done and try to love somebody and have the courage to accept the love in return.

Maya Angelou

I'm not into the money thing. You can only sleep in one bed at a time. You can only eat one meal at a time, or be in one car at a time. So I don't have to have millions of dollars to be happy. All I need are clothes on my back, a decent meal, and a little loving when I feel like it. That's the bottom line.

Ray Charles

You can have it all. You just can't have it all at one time.

Oprah Winfrey

When you go to a church and you see the pastor of that church with a philosophy and a program that's designed to bring black people together and elevate black people, join that church! If you see where the NAACP is preaching and practicing that which is designed to make black nationalism materialize, join the NAACP. Join any kind of organization—civic, religious, fraternal, political or otherwise—that's based on lifting . . . the black man up and making him master of his own community.

Malcolm X

When a person places the proper value on freedom, there is nothing under the sun that he will not do to acquire that freedom. Whenever you hear a man saying he wants freedom, but in the next breath he is going to tell you what he won't do to get it, or what he doesn't believe in doing in order to get it, he doesn't believe in freedom. A man who believes in freedom will do anything under the sun to acquire . . . or preserve his freedom.

Malcolm X

You don't have to be a man to fight for freedom. All you have to do is to be an intelligent human being.

Malcolm X

I refuse to accept the idea that the "isness" of man's present nature makes him morally incapable of reaching up for the "oughtness" that forever confronts him.

Martin Luther King, Jr.

We keep going back, stronger, not weaker, because we will not allow rejection to beat us down. It will only strengthen our resolve. To be successful there is no other way.

Earl G. Graves

There is nothing more tragic than to find an individual bogged down in the length of life, devoid of breadth.

Martin Luther King, Jr.

Freedom is an internal achievement, rather than an external adjustment.

Adam Clayton Powell

There is really nothing more to say—except why. But since why is difficult to handle, one must take refuge in how.

Toni Morrison

For in the end, freedom is a personal and lonely battle; and one faces down fears of today so that those of tomorrow might be engaged.

Alice Walker

No matter how far a person can go, the horizon is still way beyond you.

Zora Neale Hurston

I made a commitment to completely cut out drinking and anything that might hamper me from getting my mind and body together. And the floodgates of goodness have opened up on me—spiritually and financially.

Denzel Washington

Both tears and sweat are salty, but they render a different result. Tears will get you sympathy; sweat will get you change.

Jesse Jackson

It's not the load that breaks you down, it's the way you carry it.

Lena Horne

The key to success is to keep growing in all areas of life— mental, emotional, spiritual, as well as physical.

Kareem Abdul-Jabbar

Fear is a disease that eats away at logic and makes man inhuman.

Marian Anderson

Accomplishments have no color.

Leontyne Price

If you want to accomplish the goals of your life, you have to begin with the spirit.

Oprah Winfrey

There is never time in the future in which we will work out our salvation. The challenge is in the moment; the time is always now.

James Baldwin

You show me a capitalist, and I'll show you a bloodsucker.

Malcolm X

You don't make progress by standing on the sidelines, whimpering and complaining. You make progress by implementing ideas.

Shirley Chisholm

Surround yourself with only people who are going to lift you higher.

Oprah Winfrey

Imagine what a harmonious world it could be if every single person, both young and old, shared a little of what he is good at doing.

Quincy Jones

Nonviolence is the answer to the crucial political and moral questions of our time; the need for mankind to overcome oppression and violence without resorting to oppression and violence. Mankind must evolve for all human conflict a method which rejects revenge, aggression, and retaliation. The foundation of such a method is love.

Martin Luther King, Jr.

We must not, in trying to think about how we can make a big difference, ignore the small daily differences we can make which, over time, add up to big differences that we often cannot foresee.

Marian Wright Edelman

Health nuts are going to feel stupid someday, lying in hospitals dying of nothing.

Redd Foxx

The good neighbor looks beyond the external accidents and discerns those inner qualities that make all men human and, therefore, brothers.

Martin Luther King, Jr.

How far you go in life depends on your being tender with the young, compassionate with the aged, sympathetic with the striving, and tolerant of the weak and the strong—because someday you will have been all of these.

George Washington Carver

Gray hair is God's graffiti.

Bill Cosby

The price one pays for pursuing any profession, or calling, is an intimate knowledge of its ugly side.

James Baldwin

Avoid having your ego so close to your position that when your position falls, your ego goes with it.

Colin Powell

All men are caught in an inescapable network of mutuality.

Martin Luther King, Jr.

The hope of a secure and livable world lies with disciplined nonconformists who are dedicated to justice, peace, and brotherhood.

Martin Luther King, Jr.

If you cannot find peace within yourself, you will never find it anywhere else.

Marvin Gaye

We must learn to live together as brothers or perish together as fools.

Martin Luther King, Jr.

A nation or civilization that continues to produce soft-minded men purchases its own spiritual death on an installment plan.

Martin Luther King, Jr.

Injustice anywhere is a threat to justice everywhere.

Martin Luther King, Jr.

The ultimate measure of a man is not where he stands in moments of comfort, but where he stands at times of challenge and controversy.

Martin Luther King, Jr.

Indecision is like a stepchild: if he does not wash his hands, he is called dirty, if he does, he is wasting water.

African proverb

When you're poor, you grow up fast.

Billie Holiday

People who make a living doing something they don't enjoy wouldn't even be happy with a one-day work week.

Duke Ellington

Life should be lived with dignity, the personalities of others shouldn't be violated, that men should be able to confront other men without fear or shame, and that if men were lucky in their living on earth, they might win some redeeming meaning for their having struggled and suffered here beneath the stars.

Richard Wright

Unconditional love not only means I am with you, but also I am for you, all the way, right or wrong. Love is indescribable and unconditional. I could tell you a thousand things that it is not, but not one that it is. Either you have it or you haven't, there's no proof of it.

Duke Ellington

In the context of the Negro problem, neither whites nor blacks, for excellent reasons of their own, have the faintest desire to look back; but I think that the past is all that makes the present coherent, and further, that the past will remain horrible for exactly as long as we refuse to assess it honestly.

James Baldwin

The ultimate of being successful is the luxury of giving yourself the time to do what you want to do.

Leontyne Price

A man who won't die for something is not fit to live.

Martin Luther King, Jr.

There is nothing more tragic than to find an individual bogged down in the length of life, devoid of breadth.

Martin Luther King, Jr.

Everything that we see is a shadow cast by that which we do not see.

Martin Luther King, Jr.

A riot is the language of the unheard.

Martin Luther King, Jr.

An individual who breaks a law that conscience tells him is unjust, and who willingly accepts the penalty of inprison-ment in order to arouse the conscience of the community over its injustice, is in reality expressing the highest respect for the law.

Martin Luther King, Jr.

I believe that unarmed truth and unconditional love will have the final word in reality. This is why right, temporarily defeated, is stronger than evil triumphant.

Martin Luther King, Jr.

As an essayist I don't believe in the fiction of an anonymous observer. Rather than the sham of objectivity, I think you should put your perspective up front. That's only fair to the reader.

Ralph Wiley

The media's the most powerful entity on earth. They have the power to make the innocent guilty and to make the guilty in-nocent, and that's power. Because they control the minds of the masses.

Malcolm X

Hatred, which could destroy so much, never failed to destroy the man who hated, and this was an immutable law.

James Baldwin

I don't think about time. You're here when you're here. I think about today, staying in tune.

John Lee Hooker

Great careers don't come without sacrifice. Something in your life will probably have to go. Decide, now, what you're willing to forfeit to get what you want.

Cydney and Leslie Shields

I will never give in to old age until I become old. And I'm not old yet!

Tina Turner (in 1986)

Humor is laughing at what you haven't got when you ought to have it.

Langston Hughes

History is a people's memory, and without a memory, man is demoted to the lower animals.

Malcolm X

It is a blessing to die for a cause, because you can so easily die for nothing.

Andrew Young

You can't look forward and backward at the same time.

Coleman Young

There is no brilliant single stroke that is going to transform the water into wine or straw into gold.

Coleman Young

I've learned over a period of years there are setbacks when you come up against the immovable object; sometimes the object doesn't move.

Coleman Young

There are no secrets to success: Don't waste time looking for them. Success is the result of perfection, hard work, learning from failure, loyalty to those for whom you work, and persistence.

Colin Powell

A man must be willing to die for justice. Death is an inescapable reality and men die daily, but good deeds live forever.

Jesse Jackson

Love is a special word, and I use it only when I mean it. You say the word too much and it becomes cheap.

Ray Charles

The world goes on no matter what you do.

Eubie Blake

I don't know the key to success, but the key to failure is trying to please everybody.

Bill Cosby

Fame comes with its own standard. A guy who twitches his lips is just another guy with a lip twitch—unless he's Humphrey Bogart.

Sammy Davis, Jr.

There are some people that if they don't know, you can't tell them.

Louis Armstrong

Tea to the English is just a picnic indoors.

Alice Walker

Nothing ever comes to one, that is worth having, except as a result of hard work.

Booker T. Washington

Just don't give up trying to do what you really want to do. Where there's love and inspiration, I don't think you can go wrong.

Ella Fitzgerald

A man without ambition is dead. A man with ambition but no love is dead. A man with ambition and love for his blessings here on earth is ever so alive.

Pearl Bailey

I don't have any bad habits. They might be bad for other people, but they're all right for me.

Eubie Blake

Marriage is miserable unless you find the right person that is your soulmate and that takes a lot of looking.

Marvin Gaye

Poor people are allowed the same dreams as everyone else.

Kimi Gray

America will tolerate the taking of a human life without giving it a second thought. But don't misuse a household pet.

Dick Gregory

When you become senile, you won't know it.

Bill Cosby

Freedom was something internal. The outside signs were just signs and symbols of the man inside. All you could do was to give the opportunity for freedom and the man himself must make his own emancipation.

Zora Neale Hurston

Dope never helped anybody sing better or play music better or do anything better. All dope can do for you is kill you—and kill you the long, slow, hard way.

Billie Holiday

I will not take "but" for an answer.

Langston Hughes

Money it turned out was exactly like sex; you thought of nothing else if you didn't have it and thought of other things if you did.

James Baldwin

Love has no awareness of merit or demerit; it has no scale by which its portion may be weighed or measured. It does not seek to balance giving and receiving. Love loves; this is its nature.

Howard Thurman

Once upon a time freedom used to be life. Now it's money.

Lorraine Hansberry

It's easy to be independent when you've got money. But to be independent when you haven't got a thing—that's the Lord's test.

Mahalia Jackson

I think Negro wives, no matter what their age or background or even their understanding of the problem, have to be terribly strong—much stronger than their white counterparts. They cannot relax, they cannot simply be loving wives waiting for the man of the house to come home. They have to be spiritual sponges, absorbing the racially inflicted hurts of their men. Yet at the same time they have to give him courage, to make him know that it is worth it to go on, to go back day after day to the humiliations and discouragement of trying to make it in the white man's world for the sake of their families. It's hard enough for a poor working white man, but a hundred times harder for a Negro.

It isn't easy to be both a sponge and an inspiration—often it doesn't leave enough room for simple love. And you both become victims of the system you are trying to fight. So I was an exploited Negro woman who was not brave enough or smart enough to make my marriage work. And he was a Negro man who, whether he admitted it or not, found me lacking. We were divorced.

Lena Horne

Life is to be lived, not controlled, and humanity is won by continuing to play in the face of certain defeat.

Ralph Ellison

The terrible represents all that hinders, all that opposes human aspiration, and the marvelous represents the triumph of the human spirit over chaos. While the terms and conditions are different and often change, our triumphs are few and thus must be recognized for what they are and preserved.

Ralph Ellison

You shouldn't hate white people. You shouldn't hate anyone. That's no way to live.

Medgar Evers

When you clench your fist, no one can put anything in your hand, nor can your hand pick anything up.

Alex Haley

Be black, shine, aim high.

Leontyne Price

We cannot think of uniting with others, until after we have first united among ourselves. We cannot think of being acceptable to others until we have first proven acceptable to ourselves. One can't unite bananas with scattered leaves.

Malcolm X

There is nothing essentially wrong with power. The problem is American power is unequally distributed.

Martin Luther King, Jr.

A man dies when he refuses to stand up for that which is right. A man dies when he refuses to take a stand for that which is true.

Martin Luther King, Jr.

The ultimate weakness of violence is that it is a descending spiral, begetting the very thing it seeks to destroy. Instead of diminishing evil, it multiplies it.

Martin Luther King, Jr.

It may get me crucified, I may even die. But I want it said even if I die in the struggle that "He died to make men free."

Martin Luther King, Jr.

Now is the time to make real the promise of democracy, and transform our pending national elegy into a creative psalm of brotherhood. Now is the time to lift our national policy from the quicksand of racial injustice to the solid rock of human dignity.

Martin Luther King, Jr.

I have a dream that one day this nation will rise up and live out the true meaning of its creed: "We hold these truths to be self-evident; that all men are created equal."

I have a dream that one day on the red hills of Georgia the

sons of former slaves and the sons of former slaveowners will be able to sit down together at the table of brotherhood. . . .

I have a dream that my four little children will one day live in a nation where they will not be judged by the color of their skin but by the content of their character.

I have a dream today.

I have a dream that one day every valley shall be exalted, every hill and mountain shall be made low, the rough places will be made plains, and the crooked places will be made straight, and the glory of the Lord shall be revealed, and all flesh shall see it together.

Martin Luther King, Jr.

Hope is a delicate suffering.

LeRoi Jones (Amiri Baraka)

If you are afraid to die, you will not be able to live.

James Baldwin

To demand freedom is to demand justice. When there is no justice in the land, a man's freedom is threatened. Freedom and justice are interdependent. When a man has no protection under the law, it is difficult for him to make others recognize him.

James Cone

Humor is when the joke is on you but hits the other fellow first—because it boomerangs. Humor is what you wish in your secret heart were not funny, but it is, and you must laugh. Humor is your unconscious therapy.

Langston Hughes

One does not glorify in romanticizing revolution. One cries.

Lorraine Hansberry

A man is born with all the wisdom he needs for life.

Dick Gregory

I'm for truth, no matter who tells it.

Malcolm X

Truth is the baby of the world, it never gets old.

Dick Gregory

If you see somebody winning all the time, he isn't gambling, he's cheating.

Malcolm X

Let us all hope that the dark clouds of racial prejudice will soon pass away and the deep fog of misunderstanding will be lifted from our fear-drenched communities and in some not-too-distant tomorrow the radiant stars of love and brotherhood will shine over our great nation with all their scintillating beauty.

Martin Luther King, Jr.

True peace is not merely the absence of tension, but the presence of justice and brotherhood.

Martin Luther King, Jr.

I try to keep my humor away from the specific "black" and make it pertain to the general "human."

Bill Cosby

The trick is to accept what makes you good.

James Baldwin

You must be willing to suffer the anger of the opponent, and yet not return anger. No matter how emotional your opponents are, you must remain calm.

Martin Luther King, Jr.

Anyone who thinks that he can stop a natural revolution by means of repression should muster all the National Guardsmen that he can find, tell them to cross a pregnant woman's legs, and see if they can stop the baby from being born.

Dick Gregory

Injustice anywhere is a threat to justice everywhere. We are caught in an inescapable network of mutuality, tied in a single garment of destiny. Whatever affects one directly affects all indirectly.

Martin Luther King, Jr.

Anytime you see someone more successful than you are, they are doing something that you aren't.

Malcolm X

When you and I develop . . . anger, then we'll get some kind of respect and recognition, and some changes from these people who have been promising us falsely already for far too long.

Malcolm X

Just like you can buy grades of silk, you can buy grades of justice.

Ray Charles

All the money in the world will not buy you a kid who will do homework, or maturity for a kid who needs it. It may buy a kid who knows how to buy.

Bill Cosby

One of the more unprofitable strategies we could ever adopt is to join in history's oldest and most shameful witch hunt, anti-Semitism. It is nonsense to divert attention from who it is that really oppresses Negroes in the ghetto. Ultimately, the real oppressor is white American immorality and indifference and we will be letting off the real oppressor too easily if we now concentrate our fulminations against a few Jews. . . . To engage in anti-Semitism is to engage in self-destruction.

Bayard Rustin

Women, if the soul of the nation is to be saved, I believe that you must become its soul.

Coretta Scott King

We stand in life at midnight; we are always on the threshold of a new dawn.

Martin Luther King, Jr.

Hatred and bitterness can never cure the disease of fear, only love can do that. Hatred paralyzes life; love releases it. Hatred confuses life; love harmonizes it. Hatred darkens life; love illuminates it.

Martin Luther King, Jr.

In real love, you want the other person's good. In romantic love, you want the other person.

Margaret Anderson

It is the man farthest down who is most active in getting up.

Alain Locke

If Paul Robeson had not been there, I would not be here. And so it is with the youth of today. The stand you took will help us with a stand in the days, weeks, months, and years ahead, for peace, for the rights and needs of the people.

Sidney Poitier

Love is like playing checkers. You have to know which man to move.

"Moms" Mabley

The man who views the world at fifty the same as he did at twenty has wasted thirty years of his life.

Muhammad Ali

I believe this is God's island, and ultimately He will make it right.

Stevie Wonder

My first marriage was a good one, but sometimes you come to a dead end and you have to let go. Letting go is love, too, you know.

Bobby Womack

Marilyn Monroe and I discussed it often and agreed it would be nice if we could be strong enough in ourselves as women and not just there to make the male audience want to go to bed with us.

Lena Horne

Love is like a virus. It can happen to anybody at any time.

Maya Angelou

Exercise the right to dream. You must face reality—that which is. But then dream of the reality that ought to be, that must be. Live beyond the pain of reality with the dream of a bright to-morrow. Use hope and imagination as weapons of survival and progress. Use love to motivate you and obligate you to serve the human family.

Jesse Jackson

Even in our fractured state, all of us count and fit somewhere. We have proven that we can survive without each other. But we have not proven that we can win or make progress without each other. We must come together.

Jesse Jackson

I am not tragically colored. There is no great sorrow dammed up in my soul nor lurking behind my eyes. . . . I do not belong to the sobbing school of Negrohood who hold that nature some-how has given them a lowdown dirty deal and whose feelings are hurt about it. No, I do not weep at the world—I am too busy sharpening my oyster knife.

Zora Neale Hurston

Black Americans must begin to accept a larger share of respon-sibility for their lives. I don't believe that we will produce strong soldiers by moaning about what the enemy has done to us.

Jesse Jackson

We will build a democratic America in spite of undemocratic Americans. We have rarely worried about the odds or the obstacles before—we will not start worrying now. We will have both of our goals—peace and power!

Shirley Chisholm

Service is the rent you pay for room on this earth.

Shirley Chisholm

White folks don't want peace; they want quiet. The price you pay for peace is justice. Until there is justice, there will be no peace or quiet.

Jesse Jackson

If you raise up truth, it's magnetic. It has a way of drawing people.

Jesse Jackson

I'm not crazy for pretty men. Beauty in a man is not a weakness of mine.

Tina Turner

You don't have a man, you need spaghetti.

Oprah Winfrey

1. Don't live your life to please other people.
2. Don't depend on externals to help you get ahead.

3. Strive for the greatest possible harmony and compassion in your business and your life.
4. Get rid of all the back-stabbers around you.
5. Be nice, not catty.
6. Get rid of your addictions.
7. Surround yourself with people who are as good or better than you are.
8. If you're in it to make money, forget it.
9. Never give up your power to another person.
10. Don't give up.

> *Oprah Winfrey (her ten commandments for a successful life offered during her keynote address for the 1989 conference of the American Woman's Economic Development Corporation)*

I hope never to be at peace. I hope to make my life manageable, and I think it's fairly manageable now. But, oh, I would never accept peace. That means death.

Jamaica Kincaid

[In managing a business] you have to surround yourself with people you trust, and people that are good. But they also have to be people who will tell the emperor you have no clothes.

Oprah Winfrey

This medium of television is so powerful and has the ability to empower people and affect lives in such a way that you really have to have the intention to do more than just not do harm. But the intention has to be to do some good. So, I changed the way I thought about television, and decided I was more than just a talk show host, even though that's what they call me. That it was indeed a way of being a voice to the world, a way of allowing whatever I felt and the people I surrounded myself with felt, to empower, uplift, enlighten, encourage, and if we can entertain you, we're glad to do that too.

Oprah Winfrey

Let's abandon the "if it bleeds, it leads" news philosophy of the past. Enough of the body bags, ballistic tests, and bizarre crime scenes. If you repeat a problem, the problem only gets repeated.

We really ought to ask ourselves, "Do we want our children to spend hours viewing the images we're putting on the tube these days? Do we want our children influenced by visions of death and destruction, carnage and car crashes, sex and scandals?"

Sure, we can ease our consciences by telling ourselves that all of this devastation and ugliness falls under the heading of news, of the public's right, need, and desire to know. But shouldn't we also ask this: "What effect are these images having on our children, and do they really give today's youth a realistic picture of the world?"

Oprah Winfrey

If you are unhappy with anything—your mother, your wife, your job, your boss, your car—whatever it is bringing you down, get rid of it.

Tina Turner

Responsibility is one of those ten-dollar words tossed around us as lightly as love and free sex. Think about that—free sex! Nothing is free these days, and certainly not sex.

Nikki Giovanni

If you set out to be successful, then you already are.

Katherine Dunham

The only thing that will stop you from fulfilling your dreams is you.

Tom Bradley

All the money in the world doesn't mean a thing if you don't have time to enjoy it.

Oprah Winfrey

For a while in your life, you worry about the passage of time and getting old and so forth, and after a while you just say, "My God, does it matter?"

Bobby Short

To be successful as a black man in this country, you have to be bicultural. White people can function in a white world and only concern themselves with white things. But a black man has to know it all.

Arsenio Hall

If you're black and walk into a place where everybody's speaking French, *run* in the opposite direction.

Oprah Winfrey

Success is the result of perfection, hard work, learning from failure, loyalty, and persistence.

Colin Powell

If you're going to die, die doing what you love to do.

Bernard Shaw

He's my husband, my companion, my lover, my confidant. But not my focus. I wasn't lost and then found Arne. I was single and met a wonderful man and we enjoyed each other's company . . . so it was not lost and found. That's crap.

Diana Ross

The most exciting men in my life have been the men who have never taken me to bed. One can lose a great friend by going to bed with them.

Eartha Kitt

My blackness has never been in my hair. Blackness is not a hairstyle.

Bertha K. Gilkey

Truth is a theory that is constantly being disproved. Only lies, it seems, go on forever.

Eartha Kitt

Who's raising black men in this country? Black women. So if black men are not being very conscious of black women then it is our fault.

Bertha K. Gilkey

I have always thought that narcotics should be legalized so that it wouldn't be that much of a street problem.

Miles Davis

Without money, you have no control. Without control, you have no power.

Spike Lee

We need to haunt the halls of history and listen anew to the ancestor's wisdom.

Maya Angelou

Great fringe benefits come with the approach of senior citizenship. Young people defer to you, presuming that your age has brought you great wisdom. And older people smile at you because you, like them, have been around, outliving wars, earthquakes, scourges, and pestilence.

Earl G. Graves

Sex and racism have always been tied together. Look at the thousands of black men who got lynched and castrated. The reason the Klan came into being was to protect white southern women.

Spike Lee

I don't support the legalization of drugs. But . . . should we study the issue, should we consider whether decriminalization makes sense? Consider alternative ways of approaching the issue? . . . Absolutely.

Carole Moseley-Braun

Think that you, a single mother without a job, can be a success, and success will follow.

Susan Taylor

I come from a base of angry people who need me to articulate their grievances.

Al Sharpton

History is a clock that people use to tell the cultural and political time of day. It is also a compass that people use to find themselves on the map of human geography.

Dr. John Henri Clarke

I'm a full woman at fifty—full of knowledge, full of love, full of compassion. Some people get that at an earlier age, but

at fifty I'm just beginning to get it, and I'll be even better
at sixty.

Patti LaBelle

I've lived so long because I get my rest and I take my time. The
one thing I try to tell people is to slow down, don't be in such
a rush.

Mary Thompson (118 years old)

As African-Americans, we must continue to instill in our children a desire to actively participate in the economic development of the black community.

Earl G. Graves

Blacks [must] become self-sufficient by competing politically,
educationally, and economically with Whites—while living with
racism and discrimination. The first step is self-realization—to
psychologically let White people go; the next step for Blacks in
achieving parity is to recognize complete reliance on a mercurial
government or White paternalism as counterproductive; and, finally, to start fresh with a new paradigm of self-empowerment.

Tony Brown

Our time has come. Suffering breeds character. Character
breeds faith. And in the end, faith will not disappoint.
    Our time has come. Our faith, hope, and dreams will prevail.
Our time has come. Weeping has endured for the night. And
now, joy cometh in the morning.

Our time has come. No graves can hold our body down.

Our time has come. No lie can live forever.

Our time has come. We must leave the racial battleground and come to an economic common ground and moral higher ground. America, our time has come.

We've come from disgrace to Amazing Grace, our time has come.

Jesse Jackson